*So much need is there for change of scene, new
points of view. How many notice so glorious
a phenomenon as the rising of the sun over a
familiar landscape? All that is necessary to make
any landscape visible and therefore impressive
is to regard it from a new point of view, or from
the old one with our heads upside down. Then
we behold a new heaven and earth and are born
again, as if we had gone on a pilgrimage to some
far-off holy land and had become new creatures
with bodies inverted; the scales fall from our
eyes, and in like manner are we made to see
when we go on excursions into fields and pastures
new...*

John Muir *—John of the Mountains.*

Following John Muir

Searching for Enlightenment at 10,000'

Mike Miner

Cover Photo: Evolution Valley

ISBN (13): 978-1-60414-010-1

ISBN (10): 1-60414-010-0

www.fidelipublishing.com

To 'Jack' (Susie)
my partner for 35 years
who's known me since the 6th grade
but married me anyway.

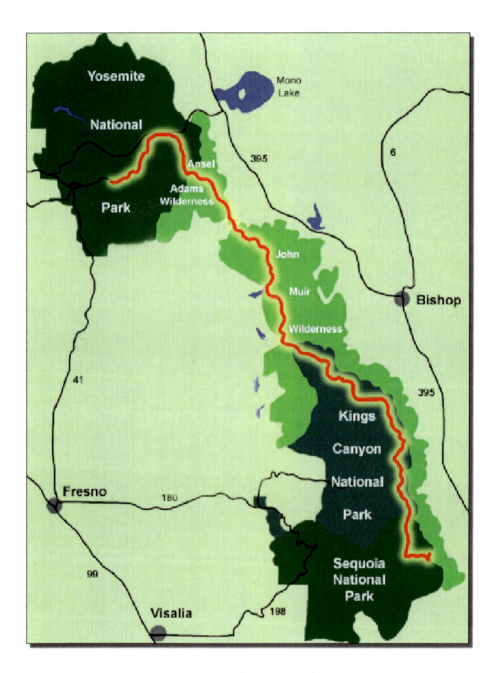

The John Muir Trail

Contents

Introduction

I'd been struggling for months trying to finish this book when I took a couple of days off work and headed up the Coast of California to go camping near Big Sur. Framed by the Pacific Ocean on one side and steep Coastal Mountains on the other side, a ribbon of asphalt called Highway 1 manages somehow to wind its way north through redwood forests and over miles of unstable mountainsides. Here all the forces of nature seem to come together and there's a sense of being connected to the Universe that is particularly strong.

I had come here seeking inspiration and had gone out for an early morning run to enjoy the solitude and try to mentally finalize the last few chapters. With a couple of miles behind me I had just settled on a concluding theme of "adversity and triumph" when I rounded a bend in the road and saw a lone figure walking in the distance. This was not normal. Nobody *walks* along Highway 1 at 6:00 a.m. In fact, it was such a curious event that I naturally assumed the Universe was trying to communicate with me, and I eagerly closed the distance between me and my intrepid messenger.

He was much older than I expected and was walking almost uncomfortably fast, despite carrying what was obviously a heavy and much used backpack. He turned as I approached, greeted me with a ready smile, and for the next mile or so we walked briskly together as he headed north. He was, it turned out, walking the length of California and had completed all but this section of the Big Sur coastline and a smaller stretch of road near San Diego. It was an interesting tale and as we continued walking together I listened intently while he told me about some of his adventures along the highways and back roads of The Golden State.

His quest was impressive to be sure, but I was still trying to hold onto my aforementioned theme. After all, I thought to myself, walking along roads hardly compares to hiking trails at 10,000 feet. We had pretty much finished talking about his current adventure when I turned the conversation toward backpacking and inquired if he had ever hiked any trails, "Let's say the John Muir Trail (JMT), for example?"

He gave me one of those knowing smiles and replied nonchalantly. "Oh sure, I hiked the JMT a few years ago when I did the Pacific Crest Trail."

"The Pacific Crest Trail? But that's more than 2,500 miles long!" I stammered.

"Yeah," he replied, "but it wasn't as hard as the Appalachian Trail."

"The Appalachian Trail? Are you kidding me!" I gasped. "How *many* trails have you hiked?"

"Well," he said slowly as he paused to consider the question. "I've done all the major trails in the U.S. (and here he began naming them off: The Continental Divide Trail, The Lewis and Clark Trail, The Potomac Heritage Trail, and so on) and a few others besides. Altogether I'd say I've hiked a little over 9,000 trail miles so far."

I was speechless, literally speechless. This guy had out-walked us by a factor of almost 50 to 1. Compared to him, our adventure on the JMT was almost inconsequential. Clearly, the Universe wasn't very impressed with our achievement, and I could see my carefully worked out theme of "adversity and triumph" lying in ruins. Another rewrite was in my future.

It was ironic how closely that chance encounter paralleled my whole JMT experience. Almost all my expectations and assumptions about spending a month backpacking in the wilderness of the High Sierras proved to be wrong. I started out sure that among all those experiences and hardships enlightenment awaited, but it never really worked out that way. I mostly got unenlightened instead.

Indeed, rather than becoming One with the Cosmos, I would begin to suspect that I had been given the male lead in *Hansel and Gretel*. The Universe, it seemed to me, had dropped little bread crumbs of wisdom all along The Trail, but I only discovered a few of them. In the end there was much that I learned, but there was more that simply left me confused.

Hiking the John Muir Trail was both an outward and an inward journey. It was the most uncomfortable thing I ever did, and our return to civilization was an occasion marked by a combination of joy and relief known to anyone who has escaped certain death. I was anxious to put the whole thing behind me and resume my "normal" life, but to my great and continuing surprise that never happened. Instead I found myself returning again and again to remembered experiences of life on The Trail and to all the questions and lessons that had been presented there with such discomforting clarity. This book is the story of those journeys.

Chapter 1

We begin from the ending

"Hello," I said into the telephone. "Is this Air San Luis? How soon can you get a plane to the Lone Pine Airport? Where is Lone Pine? About 100 miles north of Mojave. Excuse me? Is it nice here? Well, I guess if your idea of nice is watching the mercury soar into triple digits before lunch, while an absolutely endless procession of big trucks moves slowly through the middle of town on their way to and from LA, then yes this is a nice place. In fact it's a *great* place. What's that? No, I don't care how much it costs. I just want to know how *soon* you can get here. Yes. Yes, that's right. Yes. That's Great! We'll get some breakfast, and then meet you at the Lone Pine Airport in two hours. No, you won't have any trouble recognizing me. I'll be the guy with the enormous grin who's jumping up and down."

As I hung up, I turned to Susie, and together, with a smugness that neither of us was able to repress, we smiled the smile of those who have faced death by the elements, by hardship, and by the mind-numbing monotony of endless routine — and survived. It was a smile, with a smirk rising to the surface, as we realized we were about to order *anything* from a menu, after a month of eating trail mix and dehydrated food. And it was a smile, with a hallelujah buried inside, from those who many times had despaired of ever being reunited with civilization again. It was a sublime moment, and I thought back and tried to remember how it all began ...

It was a completely ordinary evening in the fall of 2003, when Susie and I began a conversation during dinner that, in hindsight, I should have been paying a *lot* more attention to. The previous year we had both turned 50, and we were talking about adventures we'd like to have before we got any older. Several ideas were presented — traveling around the world, spending a month in Spain, traveling to Asia, walking the John Muir Trail (JMT), and a few others. How and why Susie chose the JMT will forever remain "a mystery wrapped in an enigma" to me, and I must have been taking stupid pills to ever agree to such a, well, such a *stupid* idea.

What's particularly interesting about this, as I look back on it, is that it seemed like a good idea at the time. But then I suppose that's one of the prerequisites for really, really stupid ideas, and by the fourth day on The Trail, it was becoming obvious that this one was "world class." By then every muscle I possessed was sore, and small blisters were beginning to form in multiple locations. Moreover, it was becoming increasingly clear to me why it was that I never ate dehydrated food at home. Even worse, with 26 days to go, my sleeping bag was beginning to smell. In just four days it had moved from "manly," pausing briefly at "foul," and seemed intent on achieving "rancid" by week's end, and one began to suspect that this situation was unlikely to improve over time. Indeed nothing about this trip seemed likely to improve over time. But, I'm getting ahead of myself. The adventure had actually begun months before as we started preparing for what would become the most difficult and most extraordinary journey of our lives.

Chapter 2

We prepare

Throughout the winter and spring of 2004, Susie and I carefully read every backpacking review and article we could find. We collected camping gear, tested trail recipes, and began to get in shape. Soon we were regulars among the local hiking community, and friends would sometimes see us miles from home walking along the side of the road. Slowly we progressed in strength and endurance and gradually added weight to our backpacks. So, by the time of our departure we were routinely walking 10 miles and carrying about 80 lbs. between us.

By late July it was time to get all the food together that we'd need on our trip, and it was during this process that I noticed once again that Susie and I seem to think a *little* differently. I'm a visual, spatial, kind of guy, with a strong analytical finish. Susie is more of a ... more of a... well, I guess I don't really understand just what it is that Susie is more of, but it probably isn't logic and reason. Whatever the case, we were trying to determine the correct serving size of individual meals when I was once again reminded that communication is sometimes more of an art than a skill, and then there are other times when actual clairvoyance seems to be necessary. As you can see from the following conversation we had during our planning and preparation period, my normal communication skills (which I've always felt were of a superior nature) proved — not for the first time — to be mostly useless.

Susie: OK, we've got the menu planned. Now, how much of each item should we bring. ...Let's start with the vegetables.

Me: I'd say about a cup of vegetables for each meal.

Susie: I mean in ounces.

Me:	Ounces? I don't know how much a pea weighs. Let's just stick with cups.
Susie:	*(referring to her dehydrating book)* It says here that 1 oz of fresh peas will dehydrate to $^1/_4$ oz of dried peas. So, how much should we bring?
Me:	Are you talking fresh peas or dried peas?
Susie:	Don't use that tone of voice with me. Of course I mean dried peas. We're backpacking you knuckle-head.
Me:	*(attempting a different voice)* OK, so how many dried peas will it take to make a cup?
Susie:	Would you quit with the cups already. This book only talks about ounces. Now for the last time, how many ounces of peas do you want?
Me:	16
Susie:	What! You can't eat a pound of peas!
Me:	*(I started to say* "can too" *but thought better about it. At least it seemed like I was narrowing in on the correct range)* "eight ounces" *(I guessed)*
Susie:	You're just guessing!
Me:	No I'm not! *(a long pause)* ...but if I were guessing, how many ounces do you think would be a *good* guess?
Susie:	Oh, never mind!

We eventually settled on 10 ounces, which amazingly was just about right. Unfortunately, almost everything else about our food preparation was wrong. Several meals required a fry pan to cook properly, and that item was sent home early in the trip to save weight. Every breakfast and lunch consisted of oatmeal and trail mix respectively, and by the end of the first monotonous week we'd both sworn an oath that, assuming we ever got off The Trail, neither of us would eat either item for the rest of our lives. Most importantly, we completely failed to consider how many calories we'd burn each day. So, even though we packed a sufficient *quantity* of food, its overall caloric value was far less than we would need. Of course, none of this would become apparent until we were actually on the JMT, where we would each begin losing weight at the rate of about ½ lb. per day. But this rather

*30 dehydrated dinners begin to take shape on our dining room table.
These meals (along with breakfast, lunch, fuel, toiletries, etc.) were boxed
up and distributed to the various friends and family who would later
deliver them to us on one of our many re-supplies.*

significant problem was yet to be discovered, and we happily and ignorantly
continued our preparation throughout the Spring and early Summer.

    We did a little better on the gear. With a fair amount of previous
backpacking experience, some research, and lots of advice from numerous
backpacking friends, we soon began acquiring every high tech, ultralight,
camping widget we could find. Our cooking pots, stove, and even our
sporks (a combination fork and spoon) were all made of titanium, which
is lighter stronger and almost infinitely more expensive than aluminum.
Our bear canisters (the bear-proof cylinders that all our food went into)
were made from carbon fiber, and we found a company that would custom
make sleeping bags, which allowed Susie to get a bag that was just her size
(five feet tall). We were even able to add extra insulation in the foot box to

keep her feet warm.

Of course, life involves compromise, and whenever you prioritize one attribute, you're going to pay the price somewhere else. The first price we paid *was* the price because it turns out that just about everything ultralight works out to about $150 per pound! The second price was generally comfort and convenience. For example, our sporks, at $10.00 each, were undeniably light and strong, but were without a doubt the poorest excuse for an eating utensil since chopsticks. They didn't do anything well, unless you enjoyed the way soup dribbled down your chin, when the prongs of the fork-part let most of the soup leak out of the spoon-part.

The most direct compromise was our sleeping pads. Here every ½" of thickness added about one pound of extra weight and we both agonized over that equation. Eventually, we each settled on self-inflating therm-a-rest pads that were just under one inch thick. They worked surprisingly well. Not because they were particularly comfortable, but rather because they were just thick enough to insulate us from the cold ground. (At the end of most days we were so exhausted from hiking that we could easily have slept on concrete.) The biggest compromise, though, was our tent. At just under two pounds it was a whopping five pounds lighter than previous tents I had carried, and I will always love it for that reason. Unfortunately, it accomplished this incredible feat by being made of ripstop nylon, impregnated with silicone, which meant that each night all the moisture from our breathing and perspiration would condense on the inside walls of the tent and begin to "rain" down on the occupants. It was like living inside a terrarium and every morning, before we ever moved from our sleeping bags, I would wipe down the inside of the tent with my pack towel so that we could exit without getting soaked.

Finally, I should mention our favorite item of all — our chairs. Susie found a one pound fold-up chair that, while far too small for me, fit her perfectly. I carried a one-pound accessory that turned my therm-a-rest into a quite comfortable camp chair. They were the only indulgence we allowed ourselves, and we spent many of the best and most memorable times of our entire trip resting comfortably in them at the end of the day, while we enjoyed the splendor of our surroundings.

Overall, our gear choices performed well and even though our stove got temperamental whenever the temperature was below freezing, and it was often wetter inside the tent than outside, nothing failed completely. Best of all, whenever something really had to work, it did. By late July there was the predictable flurry of activity as we finished packing everything up and organized all our meals into the various boxes, which would later be packed into us by faithful friends and family on one of our five food drops. Lastly, we completed all the necessary domestic arrangements, and on Sunday, August 1, 2004, left for our great adventure, sure in the hope that our family, home, professions, and the dog would be safely waiting for us until we saw them again in September.

Chapter 3

We hit The Trail

Our itinerary called for us to start the JMT at its northern end in Yosemite Valley. There we would meet our oldest daughter, Amy, and two of her close friends, Hannah and Alisha, all of whom would accompany us on the first leg of our trip to Tuolumne Meadows. We arrived in Yosemite early and spent the time, before the girls' arrival, purchasing last minute necessities, enjoying the amenities offered by our hotel, getting trail information from the Rangers, and reading the last paper we'd see for a month. We should have skipped the last two.

The Rangers, who I had always imagined as being direct descendants of Daniel Boone — rugged and fearless individuals ready for adventure — now seemed strangely subdued and absolutely obsessed by bears. The only thing any of them wanted to talk about was an endless series of scary stories all of which featured bears, who were cunning, powerful, and carnivorous. There were stories of bears eating Top Raman still boiling in the pan, and, if you were small and lagged behind your group, bears that took packs right off your back (Susie paid particular attention to that one). And, my favorite: stories of bears that could tell what was inside a tin can. When I asked one Ranger if he thought the bears could smell through metal or were simply reading the labels, he declined to say, but remained resolute in his belief.

I'm afraid that Susie found this information somewhat disquieting, but was trying to take it in stride, when she happened to see the feature article on the front page of the Fresno Bee. The headline screamed something about Packs of Wild Bears Invade West Coast. The article went on to describe how bears were becoming increasingly aggressive and destructive. There were reports of bears in cars, bears in living rooms, and bears opening refrigerators and helping themselves. All in all it was really too much, and on the eve of our departure Susie was beginning to panic as she imagined countless numbers of bears lying in wait all along the JMT ready to help themselves to *her.*

Fortunately, before our newfound fear of bears completely overwhelmed us both, the girls showed up. Visions of being dismembered and slowly devoured by these supernatural creatures were replaced by reunions, dinner, and last-minute preparations. The next morning we ate a hearty breakfast of real food, donned our packs, and with unbridled enthusiasm hit the trail. It was a slow start. The JMT actually begins at Happy Isles, which is about a mile from where we were able to park the car. Worse, the signs direct the unwary hiker toward a beautifully maintained trail with numerous unmarked forks that all eventually lead to either dead ends or a washed out bridge.

A few hundred yards after beginning the JMT we came across our first mile marker. Only 211 miles to go!

After an hour of unwilling exploration we finally found the actual (and completely unmarked) entrance to the JMT. We were a little disheartened to learn so early in our adventure that neither our maps nor the trail signs could be trusted, but we were still maintaining a good deal of enthusiasm as we began our long ascent toward Cathedral Pass. By late afternoon it had all given way to exhaustion. We had hiked seven miles, gained 3,000 feet, and between us we had enough headaches, blisters, and aching muscles so that no one in the group felt left out. The next morning the girls left early to climb Half Dome — a very strenuous five mile side trip. Susie and I, who were both too tired and sore to move, feigned indifference explaining that we'd-been-there-done-that on a previous trip, and besides somebody needed to stay in camp to protect all the gear from marauding bears.

It was a pathetic excuse, but we were both too exhausted to care and the girls politely refrained from comment. By the time they returned it was late afternoon, and, although standing on top of Half Dome had left them exhilarated, the five mile hike and the 1,500 foot vertical climb had removed most of the swagger in their step. Nevertheless, we all donned our packs and continued our ever upward climb on the JMT eager to put some miles behind us. But, with the trail rising steeply in front of us and the sun falling toward the horizon behind us, eagerness left early, skipped right over quiet resolve, and in less than three miles arrived at submission. By the end of the second day we'd only covered a total of just over nine miles on the JMT. It wasn't an impressive beginning, but we consoled ourselves that night with our best (and heaviest) dessert Jell-O instant cheesecake — went to bed early and instantly fell asleep.

The next morning we hit the trail early and reached our first pass by 10 a.m. Finally, the trail leveled out, spirits improved, the miles fell behind us, and by evening of Day 3 we were back on schedule and comfortably camped at spectacular Cathedral Lake. With aptly named Cathedral Peak in the background, this area is one of the most photographed places in the Sierras and for good reason: towering granite peaks, a meandering stream, green meadows, and a high alpine lake all combine to make this such a breathtakingly beautiful area that even I had a difficult time not taking a great picture.

Susie and the girls telling stories and sharing Jell-O Instant Cheesecake for dessert.

Chapter 4

The girls depart

Day 4 saw our group happily hiking downhill and entering Tuolumne Meadows. This was the end of the trail for the girls and the point where Susie and I would turn south toward Red's Meadow. There, five days and almost 40 miles further down The Trail, we would hopefully meet up with my brother, Steve, and his family, along with our next re-supply of food and gear.

But first we needed to faithfully follow the JMT as it wandered somewhat aimlessly through Tuolumne Meadows. We eventually arrived at Soda Springs, where we stopped just long enough for Alisha and Susie to sample its awful tasting, mineral-laced, hot-carbonated water. The rest of us had tried the foul-tasting stuff on earlier trips, and didn't feel the need to relive that experience. So, after lots of spitting by our new tasters, we got back on The Trail for the short walk to Hwy. 120 where our car and the best (and only) hamburger stand on the JMT were waiting for us.

While the girls ordered lunch, I retrieved their car and our first re-supply package, both of which we'd previously shuttled to the nearby Ranger Station parking lot. Next, with great relief and some ceremony, Amy threw away her hiking boots. Amy likes the familiar and her boots had been familiar companions for 10 years! She'd used them on her first trans-Sierra backpack trip when she was 16 years old and on every hike since. They were old and reliable, but at Cathedral Pass they had suddenly expired. The soles delaminated, the uppers split, and poor Amy ended up with blisters on both heels. It had been painful going, and all the way down to Tuolumne Meadows there had been much cursing of her old boots and the duct tape that was holding them together.

After the boot funeral, we quickly settled down to an absolutely wonderful meal of greasy cheeseburgers and fries. Frankly, it could have been liver and onions or meat loaf surprise. The important point was that we were eating food that had been *real* food all of its life. It had never been dehydrated or freeze dried (a processes that removes most of the weight and, sadly, ALL of the flavor from any food).

(l to r) *Amy, Hannah and Alisha at Cathedral Pass*

We lingered as long as possible, but Susie and I knew we needed to get back on The Trail and put some miles behind us before evening, and we began restocking our two bear canisters with food for the next five-day leg of our trip. In went 14 lbs. of pasta, trail mix, Cliff Bars, peanut butter, bagels, oatmeal, powdered milk, dehydrated vegetables, and, what would prove to be our absolute favorite, a can of Spam. To this we added a few more pounds of dried fruit, jerky, tea, pudding, hot chocolate, toilet paper and fuel. Altogether we packed enough to go to Red's Meadow and back again. Our packs were bulging, but we were still, by JMT standards, young and dumb, and, on this second leg of our trip, we somehow found room for another three pounds of useless accessories that were never used.

It was the last time we over packed. Before the end of the trip we were planning our food consumption down to the ounce and had jettisoned every nonessential item. Between us we would shave off more than 10 lbs. from our average pack load (not to mention the more than 15 lbs. of body fat we were each destined to lose) but that was still in our unknown future and when we left Tuolumne Meadows our packs weighed more than at any other time of the entire journey.

While the girls stuffed their backpacks into the car for their drive back to civilization, we found the first of only two pay phones on the JMT and called our youngest daughter, Bethany. It was difficult to determine who was more relieved, Susie at hearing Bethany's voice or Bethany at hearing ours and realizing that we were still alive. It was a short conversation and we promised to see her in 10 days at Lake Edison, where she would drive in with her sister and Aunt to meet us for our third re-supply. We gave her our love, promised we'd call at Red's Meadow, and said good-bye.

By now Susie was nearing meltdown, which she did every time we said good-bye to *anyone*. Good byes are always difficult for her and she still had three to go. Amy, Hannah and Alisha were all excited for us, happy to have been part of the trip and thrilled beyond measure that they would be taking hot showers and sleeping in their own beds in a matter of hours. Susie finally choked out tearful farewells, secretly convinced that with 210 miles and 26 more trail days to go she was never going to see any of them again.

Finally, I promised Amy I'd take good care of her mother and that we'd arrive safely at Lake Edison. With that assurance the girls drove away, and we hoisted our packs and started walking south. We were both a bundle of conflicting emotions: sad to leave loved ones behind, anxious with the knowledge that more than 200 miles and seven major passes[1] lay in front

---

[1]Because the JMT mostly follows the ridgeline of the Sierra Nevada Mountains, we hiked over passes almost every day. Most of these were in the 10,000' range, but there are seven major passes over 11,000'. (See Trail Profile page 144-145)

of us, but excited as little kids on their first trip to Grandma's house. We had planned this trip together and knew that we were going to succeed or fail as a couple. For the first time we were alone on the JMT, and we were eager to discover what adventures awaited us.

Chapter 5

We're on our own

From Tuolumne Meadows the JMT heads south, crosses the Tuolumne River and enters Lyell Canyon, one of the most beautiful valleys in the Sierra Nevada and another example of why Yosemite National Park is such a visual jewel. The trail hugs the western edge of the valley as it slowly rises to meet the base of Donahue Pass. We hiked until late afternoon and made camp on a small hill that afforded a wonderful view of the entire valley. To the south and east lay the headwaters of the Tuolumne River, as well as our first major pass and the eastern boundary of Yosemite National Park. Just below us we watched the river flow gently northward through the meadow of Lyell Canyon and on to Tuolumne Meadows. It was gorgeous!

We dropped our packs and walked down to the river to enjoy a quick bath. Here I should mention that I'm using "enjoy" and "bath" in a sense not usually associated with those words. Trying to produce the same effect at home would require the following conditions: 1) stand naked in your back yard whenever the temperature is no more than 50 degrees and the weather is such that the moment you get wet the sun will slip behind a cloud and the wind will pick up; 2) find an area that's not level, has lots of rocks and sharp twigs, and some slippery mud or moss so that every step will be both painful and dangerous; 3) have a large body of cold water nearby and add several 50 lb. blocks of ice to simulate a river being fed by melting snow; 4) use a 1½ qt. saucepan to clean and rinse with (the <u>same</u> saucepan you'll later use to cook dinner); 5) provide one very thin hand towel to dry yourself off and 6) practice hyperventilating while screaming "Eeee-oooo-wwww!!!" uncontrollably *every time* you pour water on yourself.

In actual fact our real bathing ritual, which we endured on a daily basis, was usually worse. The goal, of course, was to get as clean as possible, as quickly as possible, while trying to prevent all the soap and gunk from getting back in whatever lake or river we were standing next to. So, stripping to our underwear[2] we each filled a pot with water, added a few drops of biodegradable soap, stepped back from the water's edge and began to scrub. The "soaping" process usually required three pots of water — one for the lower half, one for the upper half, and one for head and hair. Next it was time to rinse, and three more potfuls of icy cold water were quickly poured over head and body. By this time our teeth were chattering and we each had goose bumps the size of golf balls. We quickly dried off with our tiny backpack towels (essentially a chamois that you dried with, wrung out, and dried some more) then put on clean underwear and socks, a pair of sweat pants, and every sweater and jacket we had.

Of course, I'm once again taking great liberties with words — in this case the word "clean." Throughout the trip we carried two sets of clothes each, the ones we were wearing and a second set in our pack. Pants might be worn for days, but the T-shirt, underwear, and socks we had worn that day were rinsed out each afternoon and hung out to dry. If it rained or froze that night (or both) the damp clothes would be strapped to the outside of our packs to dry as we hiked along the trail. While this process never produced "spring fresh" laundry, it did prevent our clothes from actually getting up and running away.

Our next job was to replenish our water supply. While many die-hard backpackers drink water straight out of any stream available, we belonged to the more cautious majority that pumped all water through a filter that removed every bacterium, protozoa, and amoebae that threatened our lower intestinal tract. Each afternoon we'd fill our entire 6-liter assortment of water containers with filtered water, which was usually enough for drinking as well as preparing dinner that night and tomorrow's breakfast.

With those daily jobs complete, we finally arrived back at our little

---

[2]At this early stage of the trip Susie wore a bathing suit, but it, along with all remaining pretenses of modesty, was sent home at our next re-supply to save weight.

campsite clean, refreshed, and with enough daylight left to sit for awhile with a cup of hot tea and enjoy the view. It was a perfect day. We had left Cathedral Lake early that morning, walked mostly downhill until lunchtime, had the best greasy cheeseburgers of our life, and then hiked the rest of the afternoon on the flattest part of the JMT we were ever to see. We made quick entries in our journals, read for a bit, then cooked dinner and decided to forget the tent and sleep under the stars. With our heads poking out of our sleeping bags, we looked up in awe at the night sky and quickly fell asleep with the sound of the river flowing gently below us.

As I dozed off, I had half expected my next journal entry to be something along the lines of, "...and they lived happily ever after." Instead, it read "...and we barely survived the night!" It turns out that Lyell Canyon is home of the cold-wind-that-blows-down-from-the-mountain-and- freezes-everything, as well as competing groups of coyotes that howled like banshees. The first call came around midnight from just across the valley, followed by more distant responses from both north and south. Within moments they were all crying back and forth in an unending series of blood curdling howls that Susie quickly interpreted as, "hey, guys there's fresh meat at the campsite down by the river."

They eventually quieted down, but we slept uneasily the rest of the night, convinced that we'd likely be eaten by morning. However, rather than waking up surrounded by a pack of wild coyotes intent on having us for breakfast, we instead awoke to an icy breeze that had deposited a thick layer of frost on everything — including us. I watched as Susie, who was completely buried inside her sleeping bag, cautiously poked just enough of her head out to take a look. She surveyed our surroundings in disbelief, convinced that we had been hit by a blizzard, and then muttered a pathetic and muffled cry as she saw the ice on top of her bag.

In life there are two kinds of people: morning people — those who awaken "bright-eyed and bushy-tailed" ready and eager to face the day — and everyone else. Susie is not of the first kind. To her the first 30-plus minutes of morning are a time of great unpleasantness even under the best of circumstances. If you have to get out of bed and get dressed when it's literally freezing, the whole experience becomes almost unbearably impossible to deal with. Thus it was on the morning in question.

I was up, dressed, mostly packed, and preparing breakfast by the time Susie had finally summoned up enough resolve to face the day. She carefully reached one hand out and retrieved her clothes bag, which was nearby and covered in frost. Next she got up and stood on top of her sleeping bag dressed only in pajamas and a stocking cap. Tragically, she had failed to fully anticipate her next move, which was to remove either the top or bottoms of her pajamas and replace them with the frozen hiking clothes in her bag. It was a hard decision with only bad choices. Fortunately, after some cursing and much whining she eventually saved her life by settling on an action plan.

We quickly ate, packed up, and headed down the trail. It was the last time we ever slept outside. From then on we pitched our tent every night. Intellectually we knew the walls of the tent weren't much thicker than Saran Wrap, and the only thing it could protect us from was rain and the smaller less aggressive members of the insect kingdom, but, just like the forts we all built when we were kids, it *felt* safe when you were inside.

Leaving our "coyote campsite" behind, we followed The Trail south as it began a gradual rise to meet the base of Donahue Pass. We made good time and stopped early that afternoon to camp at a picturesque lakelet about 2,000 feet below the summit. Here the terrain briefly flattened out and the headwaters of the Tuolumne River formed several pools of varying size each as lovely as the next. It was easy to find a great campsite and we spent a long afternoon comfortably seated outside our little tent while enjoying the view and a shared treat of tea and cookies.

Leaving early the next morning, we hiked past what is left of Lyell Glacier. In the last Ice Age this once mighty glacier had formed Lyell Canyon, but today only a few acres of snow and ice survive. As global warming continues, it is expected to cease to exist altogether within the next decade.

We continued ever upward, finally reaching the top of Donahue Pass by midday, where we stopped for a long and well-deserved break. This summit marked the southernmost boundary of Yosemite National Park and the first of the seven major passes over 11,000 feet that we would have to climb before the end of the JMT. In front of us lay the Ansel Adams Wilderness. Far below we could see pieces of the trail wind its way south, and in the far distance, distinctive, pyramid shaped, Silver Peak rose up to meet the horizon.

It was a sobering view — magnificent to be sure, but the sheer distances were staggering! From here we could see almost 100 miles down the spine of the Sierra Nevada Mountains as countless valleys and peaks marched southward. Getting to the horizon across those barriers seemed impossible in itself, but that distance represented only the <u>first half</u> of our journey. Beyond the horizon, beyond the limit of our vision, lay more than 100 *additional* miles of the JMT and *six* more major passes.

It was a thoroughly depressing moment and I wondered, not for the last time, how I'd ever let myself get talked into this trip. In full self pity mode I began to take stock. Somewhere I'd read that the human foot has more than 100 different bones and muscles, and after eight days on the trail *every* one of mine hurt. In fact, I remember thinking that about the only part of my body that didn't hurt were my ears, and they were beginning to freeze

Beautiful Lyell Canyon with Donohue Pass in the distance

in the icy wind. Even worse, what I'd hoped were allergies had by now turned into a bad cold. I knew I should be home in bed with some chicken noodle soup, but that wasn't on my list of options. Actually, *nothing* was on my list of options except following Susie down the trail, which in another three days would bring us to Red's Meadows, where, hopefully, family and food would be waiting.

Chapter 6

On to Red's Meadow

Throughout that morning the weather continued to warm, and, with the next few miles almost all downhill, my mood steadily improved. About noon we stopped beside a quiet and secluded little stream where we soaked our feet, ate lunch, replenished our water supply and hung out just long enough for me to have my first epiphany.

Having now struggled over two passes and more than 40 miles of trail, not to mention six days of dehydrated trail food, and five nights in a sleeping bag that was beginning to reek, I was surprised to realize how utterly content I felt at the moment. More surprising still was the very short and simple list that was at the root of my contentment: I was warm, I was eating, I had taken my boots off, and, most wonderful of all, my 45 lb. pack was resting comfortably on the ground instead of on *me*.

Each of these conditions was a sensational improvement over my normal and everyday routine of life-on-the-trail, but the really astonishing fact was that, compared to my "real" life back home, these were all *expected* conditions. It was a powerful affirmation of the old cliché that "in the end it really doesn't take much to be happy." Of course, this sudden illumination failed to fully account for the obvious and unpleasant fact that for the next 23 days I wasn't going to *have* much. Worse yet it completely ignored the basic problem that each and every one of the unpleasant conditions I had just identified were all rather necessary components of actually hiking the JMT, which I suppose is the reason that my new found sense of contentment and self-righteousness pretty much disappeared about ¼ of a mile later when we started up the next hill.

By now the foot traffic on the JMT had thinned out considerably compared to what we'd encountered in Yosemite National Park, and we saw only a few groups of fellow hikers as we hiked into the afternoon of our sixth day on The Trail. With our route continuing southwards we began to parallel the Minaret Mountains[3] to the west of us. We passed beautiful Thousand Island Lake by midday and should have stopped for the night, but instead decided to push on to Garnet Lake, which we reached by late afternoon. Quite large by Sierra standards, and at 9,678' mostly above timber line, Garnet Lake is beautifully bordered by the Minarets on the west and smaller mountains on the north and south. On the east side, the outlet crosses the JMT, where the terrain flattens out and the only decent campsites are located.

At this altitude the growing season is only about three months each year, and trees, which are sparse and grow only a few inches each year, often look like they belong in a Japanese Bonsai garden. Flowers and grasses, if they grow at all, are usually one or two inches tall compared to their one or two foot counterparts at lower elevations. All this makes high alpine lakes very sensitive to overuse, and Garnet Lake has suffered because of its popularity. Unfortunately, and to our great disappointment, we failed to anticipate this problem and upon our arrival found that the Forest Service has prohibited all camping near the outlet, and the few remaining legal sites were already taken.

We checked the map and briefly considered continuing on to the next lake, but with evening fast approaching it was too far away to make before nightfall. It looked like there might be some campsites on the northeast shore of the lake, so we followed a small footpath that led in that direction. Our hunch was correct, but other hikers had arrived before us and we found that every possible spot was occupied. Soon the path disappeared altogether and we found ourselves struggling to maintain our footing as the terrain became steeper and more rocky. As twilight neared we eventually found what was to be our worst campsite of the entire trip.

---

[3]The Minarets are a very distinctive group of jagged peaks that rise substantially above the surrounding terrain. Besides their undeniable beauty they're also one of the most easily recognizable landmarks in the Sierras.

We had located a spot that was so high above the lake that it took more than 15 minutes just to hike down and back to the lake in order to bathe and pump water. We pitched our tent on a small "flat" spot, and with no room to spare moved the "kitchen" over rocks and bushes to another "flat" spot 50 yards away where we ate dinner. With no place to sit and relax we went to bed early and, as we began to slide toward the bottom of the tent, discovered that our campsite only looked level compared to the rest of the terrain. Actually it had quite a slope to it, and we spent much of the night crawling to the top of the tent and sliding slowly down to the bottom again. Such is life on a mountainside.

We awoke early the next morning (at the bottom of the tent) and broke camp in record time. We careful picked our way back down the steep, loose terrain and finally regained the JMT just as the sunrise was lighting up Banner Peak and Mt. Ritter, both of which rise over the west end of Garnet Lake. It was an exquisite sight, with the mountains bathed in the red light of dawn and reflected perfectly in the morning calm of the lake, and I took one of my top 10 best pictures of all time. I later discovered that this is another often photographed view in the Sierras and I was pleased to see that my shot was almost the equal of the many professional prints seen in books and calendars.

We watched for several minutes as the sunrise continued to unfold. Susie pretty much summed up our feelings of Garnet Lake and its accommodations, when she commented that she'd never seen a more lovely lake nor more wretched campsites than what lay before us. The contrast was remarkable and, to our good fortune, wasn't repeated. We never had another problem with campsites for the rest of the trip. With a last look we turned away from Garnet Lake and headed south-southeast toward the rising sun and Red's Meadow.

We made good time throughout the morning and arrived at pretty Rosalie Lake about noon. The trail skirted the eastern side of the lake through a small stand of mixed pine and fir trees, while a sheer granite wall provided a backdrop across the entire western half of the lake. Surprisingly we had seen only a few hikers that day, (apparently, everyone was still at Garnet Lake) and we had the lake along with a choice of perfect picnic

Garnet Lake at sunrise

spots all to ourselves. We ate lunch as slowly as possible and laid around for another half hour trying to think of an excuse that would allow us to spend the night, but it was no use. We were scheduled to meet my brother, Steve, and his family the next morning and we still had a long way to go. So, it was back to The Trail and on to our next destination.

From here it was mostly downhill along a dusty and much-used section of trail. Our plan had been to hike about 11 miles for the day and camp at Johnston Lake, which would leave us an easy four miles to go in the morning. However, upon arriving at our intended destination we discovered that it was an unexpectedly popular spot for groups on horseback to stop and rest. This meant that it was dusty, because of overgrazing and overuse, and was full of horse manure, which produced a powerful aroma that was appreciated only by the thousands of horse flies who called the place home. Basically, it was an awful spot and with much reluctance we decided to push on to Red's Meadows, where we finally arrived almost three hours later.

It had been a grueling 15 mile day and we both limped into camp where we stopped at the first picnic table we came to. Gingerly removing our boots to search for blisters, neither of us was disappointed. Together we had a half dozen new foot blisters, and while the ones on top of Susie's toes were both impressive and unusual, my brand new heel blisters were easily in first place. They really were nasty and I would end up treating them twice a day the rest of the trip, but with Susie's nursing skills, along with a goodly helping of assorted bandages and duct tape, they never got out of control.

After our first-aid break we began a quick exploration of our surroundings. Red's Meadow was by far the busiest place we encountered throughout our entire journey on the JMT. It's a mini-town deep in the Sierras that comes alive each spring when the snows melt, and closes up each autumn. Access is via Mammoth Lakes, but, because of its popularity during the summer, private vehicles are not allowed on the narrow road. Instead visitors must leave their cars in Mammoth Lakes and take a 45 minute bus ride to Red's Meadow. Once there they can choose from six different trail heads, or enjoy a restaurant, a small motel, an even smaller grocery store, and most surprising to us a designated campground for backpackers.

After so much time in the wilderness we were both a little put out at the thought of being restricted in our choice of camp sites, but got over it the moment we discovered that the campground offered free *hot* showers. A hot shower? A free hot shower with all the hot water you wanted because it comes out of a thermal hot spring? We looked at each other and couldn't stop smiling. We dropped our packs grabbed the biodegradable soap, our "clean" clothes, and ran for the bath house. It was a wooden structure with a half dozen individual shower rooms, no lighting, and bare concrete floors. The place had definitely lost its AAA rating sometime ago, but we didn't care. Free flowing hot water was Five-Star luxury as far as we were concerned, and Susie would probably still be enjoying that shower if another waiting backpacker, who smelled as bad as we did, hadn't kept banging on the door.

We lingered as long as possible, but eventually found our way back to our designated campground where we ran into a young married couple and a father and son team, all of whom we'd repeatedly encountered on the trail since leaving Yosemite. We were all hiking the JMT, and after dinner we shared stories over dessert and the pint of wine I had carried for 27 miles. It was a wonderful evening with newfound friends, and it was profoundly comforting to hear that we weren't the only ones who had multiple blisters and aching muscles, that everyone felt the first 58 miles of the JMT had "kicked their butts," and that we were all secretly terrified of the next 160+ miles of trail that lay ahead.

Chapter 7

We meet up with the "young" Miners

The next morning we packed up our gear and walked over to the Village which included a restaurant, motel, and grocery store. Not surprisingly our first stop was the restaurant, where we left our backpacks on the porch with a dozen others and walked inside to a room full of fellow backpackers. Most of them were "newbies" who were enjoying a last hearty meal before heading out on the various trails for weekend trips. Easy to spot, they were clean shaven and wore sparkling clean clothes — even their packs were clean. We, on the other hand, presented a rather different look.

It was a look that is much easier to describe than it is to achieve. It was a look reserved for those who have put almost 60 miles of hard trail behind them, and endured eight days of nothing but trail food. It was a look for those who haven't shaved in a week, and already can't remember what shampoo smells like. Finally, it was a look of those whose pants, boots, shirt, hat and jacket looked like they had been worn continuously for a week — because they had. Altogether we had the look of a couple not to be trifled with, a couple that one would want to keep at a distance, for both physical survival and olfactory safety.

The waitress told us to sit anywhere, and when she came over to our table both of us ordered the biggest breakfast they served. We looked at each other and couldn't stop smiling. We smiled at the chairs we were sitting on and the hot coffee the waitress kept pouring. We smiled when the food arrived and smiled so much while we were eating it that our faces started to hurt. It was the most delicious breakfast ever served, and we left the restaurant with great reluctance, hoping that Steve and family would arrive late enough for us to have another meal.

In the meantime, we found some comfortable benches outside where each of us wrote postcards to the girls and dropped them into an actual mailbox — the only one on the JMT. We spent a little more time writing in our journals, and were just beginning to wonder what the restaurant would be serving for lunch when the 10 o'clock bus from Mammoth arrived, and with it Steve, his wife, Dorothy, and sons Jake, Tom and Matt. They had driven down from their home in Oregon the day before, bringing all their backpacking gear as well as one of our larger re-supply boxes (which we had previously shipped to them). Best of all, they had also brought fresh food for the day's lunch and dinner[4].

There were hugs all around and animated conversations as we tried to catch up on each other's lives. The boys, who ranged in age from 14 to 18, were changing as only teenage boys can. Since visiting them just four months earlier, we couldn't help but spot new whiskers on Jake, while Tom and Matt had both grown noticeably taller. They, of course, were all eager to hear about our adventures in the last week and listened intently as we tried to describe life on The Trail.

We spent most of the next hour talking and packing, dividing the contents of the re-supply box between Susie's and my pack, and the contents of the ice chest, which contained the fresh food for tonight's dinner, between Steve and the boys. Re-supplies were always a love-hate experience. Because we had planned carefully, almost all of our food and consumables (fuel, cooking oil, toilet paper, etc.) were nearly gone by the time each re-supply arrived, which meant that just before each re-supply our packs were light by five to 10 lbs. So, we *loved* getting all the "stuff" we needed, but we *hated* putting all that weight back in our packs.

---

[4]Months before, Steve had volunteered to provide dinner on our first night out of Red's Meadow and had asked for special requests. Knowing that we'd be sick of dehydrated trail food by then, I had responded, "I really don't care what you bring as long as it was <u>alive</u> the day before."

The plan was for Steve, Jake and Matt to join us for the next 35-mile section of the trip, which would take us all the way across the Sierras to Lake Edison. In the meantime Dorothy and their middle son, Tom, would drive around the Sierras, visit some friends in Los Angeles, and then meet us in five days.

By 11 a.m. we were packed and ready to go. We all posed for pictures by the sign at the trailhead, then waited patiently while Susie bid another tearful farewell, this time to her sister-in-law and nephew. Finally, the five of us hoisted our packs and joined the JMT as it headed south. This next section of The Trail was the same hike that Steve and I had done together almost 15 years ago. For both of us that earlier trip had been our first trans-Sierra hike, and, due to a very late winter that year, our first snow trip. It had been a great experience and we were both excited to be able to relive part of that adventure with Susie and the boys.

Chapter 8

Life with the boys

Leaving Red's Meadow The Trail starts out mostly flat, and very hot and dusty, as it meanders through a burned-out section of the forest. In about an hour it begins a moderately steep ascent, and shortly afterwards crosses a small creek and reenters the forest. It was here that we made our first stop for lunch.

Unlike breakfast and dinner, which were generally some version of a communal one-pot-meal cooked on our tiny backpack stove, lunch was left up to the individual. Each of us carried a slightly different assortment of trail mix, dried fruit, jerky, bagels, salami, cheese, peanut butter and jelly, and Cliff Bars. Each person's lunch was then stored in a single stuff bag near the top of his own pack, where it could be retrieved easily and often. "Lunch" was therefore a recurring event that began immediately after breakfast, at the first rest stop, and generally resumed at each stop thereafter. Typically, we had two short rest stops in the morning, a long stop (about 30 minutes) around noon, and one or two more short stops before making camp at the end of the day.

Imagine then at least four times a day grabbing a handful of "lunch" and eating it. And even though lunch was an assortment, it was always the *same* assortment. It never changed except to get a little staler (or later in the trip, when it started to rain, a little soggier). Now imagine reaching for lunch on that first morning out of Red's Meadow expecting the "same-o-same-o" but instead your brother starts handing out *fresh* ham sandwiches, on *fresh* bread, with *fresh* lettuce and tomatoes. WOW! He had made them all that morning, put them in the ice chest, and then carefully buried them deep in his pack to keep them cool. It was the BEST sandwich I ever had!

While we s-l-o-w-l-y ate our delicious lunch, Steve and I looked over the map and discussed the particulars of the next few days. We knew that five days would get us to Lake Edison with a comfortable margin of time to spare, but now we were planning exactly where to camp, where to fish, how many miles each day, etc. After our first quick perusal of the map we looked at each other, looked back at the map with renewed scrutiny, and then began to wonder out loud just where all those mountains that stood between us and Lake Edison had come from. They hadn't been there 15 years ago. Had they?

It turns out that after leaving Yosemite Valley, Red's Meadow is the lowest point on the entire JMT. And that of course means that when you leave Red's Meadow in *any* direction you will be going uphill; and if, like us, you happen to be following the JMT south you'll be going uphill for a very, very long time. On the map it looked like *forever*, and, as it turned out, at almost 20 miles and the better part of three days of nothing but "up," it almost was!

We tried to console ourselves with, "Well, maybe it isn't as bad as it looks." (Both of us knew it was a lie, but we went with it.) The rest of the day was slow going as we went up, up, up. Steve and the boys weren't used to the altitude, and Susie and I were exhausted from the previous day's 15-mile hike. We pushed on until mid afternoon, when, tired and footsore, we arrived quite unexpectedly at a lovely little meadow, with a stream flowing into it and a perfect campsite off to the side. We had only covered a bit less than five miles, but there was an immediate and unanimous decision to call it a day. We set up camp and by mid afternoon we were all laying on our therm-a-rests or sitting in camp chairs.

The boys had been on several previous backpack trips with me and I always tried to bring some new learning experience into each of our adventures. For example, on past trips they had learned how to build campfires, how to fish, and how to cook[5]. Unfortunately, our present campsite didn't offer a lot of opportunity to practice any of these skills. There was no lake and the stream was too small for fishing. Because of our

---

[5] The boys were actually pretty good at building fires and not bad at fishing, but they absolutely excelled at losing my fishing lures. (Last year the score was: fish caught 10, lures lost 12.) As far as cooking went they were able to boil water, which, as it happens, is about all you need to know when you're cooking dehydrated food.

altitude, campfires weren't allowed, and we wouldn't start cooking dinner for at least an hour. So, being the thoughtful uncle that I am, I suggested that now would be a good time to learn about backpacker bathing techniques.

Being good sports and completely ignorant of what the process involved[6] the boys grabbed their towels, some clean clothes (which, because this was their first day on The Trail, actually *were* clean) and followed me down to the stream's edge. I explained the basic concept — get as clean as possible while keeping as much soap and grime as possible out of the water source. They nodded with understanding, but were appalled when I began to demonstrate by pouring a pan full of freezing cold soapy water over my head. I finished my "bath" in record time and managed to keep my involuntary screaming to a minimum, but when I turned to the boys and indicated that it was their turn, I sensed a certain reluctance.

Judging by the looks on their faces I suspected they would have rather donated a kidney than have anything to do with Uncle Mike's idea of trail hygiene. So, I decided not to push my luck and left them to ponder their response while I headed back to camp. Based on the screams I later heard and the partially wet hair when they returned, my guess was that they had done a pretty good job of it. Nevertheless, the experience must have been horrifying for them because for the rest of the trip they *never* bathed again.

The next morning we continued our climb. Soon The Trail left the cover of the forest and opened up to a panoramic view of Cascade Valley. This is one of the largest valleys in the Sierras and we followed along its northern side as the trail gradually ascended to 11,000 feet. It was a long hot, and dusty section, but the views were spectacular for the rest of the day. Almost 2,000 feet below us we could see stretches of Fish Creek. Across the valley and at its western end stood Silver Peak, that ever-distinctive, pyramid-shaped mountain that we'd first seen four days ago as we left Yosemite National Park.

---

[6]The reader may wish to review Chapter 5 where bathing in the high country was discussed in detail.

We spent the night at overcrowded Purple Lake and left early the next morning. Continuing to follow the ridge trail high above Cascade Valley, we could see our next destination far away on the opposite side. Looking at the map and back again at the terrain, we knew that sometime this afternoon we were going to be treated to a first-person encounter with the bottom of Cascade Valley. In other words, we would have to climb down almost 2,000 vertical feet and then climb right back up the other side. It sucked, but by now Susie and I were getting used to the idea that this particular attribute of the high country was just as inescapable as it was unpleasant.

Every day the mountains were presenting us with lessons in the "yin and yang" of daily existence. Intellectually, most everyone understands that up-down, warm-cold, hungry-full are each fundamentally connected. You really can't experience one without the other. But in our *Everyday World* that doesn't mean we don't try. Going "up" — take an elevator. Feeling cold — turn the heater on. Hungry — order a sandwich. But, in the mountains none of that works.

If nothing else life in the high country is an in-your-face education in the Eastern philosophical concept of Duality. Here life becomes simple, <u>not easy</u>, but simple. You eat when you're hungry, sleep when you're tired, and sweat every time there is an "up." Abstractions disappear, and choices, which are generally few and always free of subtleties, are usually obvious. On The Trail life is physical not cerebral, and, while difficulties were frequent, the effects of living life simply were profound. On The Trail every drink of water was delicious, every meal was appreciated, and every night we slept like the dead.

Here I should confess that this insight and all the other epiphanies I experienced on The Trail only happened when I was walking downhill or resting. Every time I went uphill my muscles grabbed every available molecule of energy my body could produce with nothing left over for higher level brain functions. Honestly, during every ascent we made I couldn't do simple arithmetic. But today we were mostly going downhill, and that reality combined with my recent insight had produced a mood of contented self-righteousness that could only be undone by the most unusual of encounters, which, as it happened, was very quickly hiking toward us.

It was still early morning when we rounded a bend in The Trail, and far ahead we could see a lone hiker headed our way. This was hardly an unusual event, but this hiker seemed to be moving rather quickly. In fact, we soon realized, he was running! This *was* unusual. We were more than 10 miles from the nearest trailhead, so this guy wasn't out for a morning jog. By now we could see that he was carrying a small backpack, and, stranger still, as we continued to close the distance, it became obvious that our lone hiker was actually a young lady.

Although clearly in a hurry, she politely stopped as we all crowded around to gawk and ask questions. While we had read about people like her, she was our first encounter with an ultralight hiker. These hardy souls have taken backpacking to an extreme level. As their name implies, they travel light — compared to my 45 lb. load she was carrying 17 lbs! But this weight loss requires that one lead a rather Spartan lifestyle on The Trail.

First, they leave behind all the "extras:" things like sleeping bags, tents, water filters, bear canisters, and most of the kitchen. They have one set of clothes (the ones they're wearing), most meals are a combination of trail mix and energy bars, and at night they sleep on a thin foam pad, put on a layer of fleece, a jacket, and cover themselves with a tarp. The advantage is that they move <u>fast</u>. A typical ultralight backpacker will cover 20-30 miles every day! And she was no exception. Seven days ago she had started hiking the JMT at its southern terminus, Whitney Portal, and was planning on completing the <u>entire</u> JMT in a total of nine days.

Nine days! Everyone in our group continued to ask her questions, but I couldn't get past the math. For a moment I was back in high school algebra and I could hear Fr. Newman asking one of those dreadful time/distance problems...

"If a train travels 50 mph due west, and Fred rides his bike south, how much will Sara weigh when she arrives at her destination?"

Huh? Apparently I'd been walking uphill longer than I realized, because none of this was working for me. According to our schedule we had 20 days and a little more than 140 miles to go before we reached Whitney Portal, and she had just walked that entire distance in seven days! Even more unbelievably she planned just two more days to finish, because, according to her, the last portion of the trail was the easiest. Remember, this was the same 60+ mile section that we had just completed, and of all the adjectives Susie and I might have used to describe that experience, "easy" wasn't on either of our lists.

I was still trying to get my mind around all the numbers when our ultra light hiker gave us all a hasty "good bye" turned north and started *running* down the trail toward Yosemite Valley. As she disappeared around the first bend my previously described sense of contentment left with her, and was, I'm afraid, replaced by a big hole where the bulk of my manly self-confidence normally resided. Nine days for the entire JMT, I thought to myself incredulously and worse yet she was a *girl!*

By the end of the trip we would meet at least a dozen more ultra light hikers like her — two of them a couple in their 70's who were hiking the entire 2,650 mile Pacific Crest Trail. But for now we tried to find solace in the belief that she was probably a lone mutant and most likely not even from this planet. Still, we couldn't help but be "blown away" by her speed, and we must have looked rather forlorn as we trudged on toward the bottom of Cascade Valley.

We arrived there about noon and stopped at the trail junction for lunch. From here we could look out on Tully Hole, which is actually a large meadow at the extreme southern end of Cascade Valley. We had just finished eating and were quietly admiring the view when we couldn't help but notice that it had started to rain. Up until now we had enjoyed a string of sunny days, but today clouds had been building since early morning. It was becoming obvious that a cold front was moving through, and rain was going to be part of our future.

In fact, our future was about to include 12 straight days of rain! Indeed, we were in for so much rain that it would become the defining characteristic of our entire trip, and would eventually force almost every other hiker off

The Trail. But we didn't know that yet (and would certainly have joined the exodus if we had). For now we hoped it was a typical afternoon thunderstorm, and we donned our rain gear before trudging on.

We followed Fish Creek as it plunged into Cascade Valley for the next mile. The steep descent meant that there were plenty of waterfalls to admire, but it also meant that all this lost altitude would have to be regained tomorrow.

Finally, the JMT turned left and crossed Fish Creek. From here The Trail began a steep ascent toward Silver Pass, which was about five miles away and, worse by far, almost one mile straight up! It was a distressing thought and with the rain still coming down, we decided to camp here and tackle the climb in the morning.

We quickly pitched our tents and climbed inside to wait out the storm. Fortunately, because nothing is more torturous for teenage boys than to be trapped inside a tent all afternoon, the rain proved to be light and intermittent. So, with Susie content to lay comfortably in our tent and read, the rest of us grabbed a tiny deck of cards and headed for a nearby rocky ledge that overlooked Fish Creek and its waterfalls. From here we spent the better part of a delightful afternoon admiring the scenery, while the boys taught Steve and me every weird card game they knew.

We got an early start the next morning, but the climb up to Silver Pass was every bit as brutal as the topo map[7] showed it to be. By noon we were nearing the summit from the north as a major thunderstorm was approaching stealthily from the south. Not uncommon in the High Sierras, these thunderstorms begin in the Central Valley of California, where the air is hot and full of moisture. As this air mass pushes against the Sierra Nevada Mountains, it quickly rises where it is met by the much colder mountain air. The result is often an enormous black cloud, called a thunderhead, which can rise to over 40,000 feet. They're beautiful to

---

[7] "Topo" short for topographical. All the maps we carried contained contour lines, with each line representing an 80' change in elevation. So, the closer the lines the steeper the grade. Here the lines mostly touched -a bad sign!

look at, but inside these behemoths are forces that ultimately produce lightning: those million-volt flashes of electrical energy that have a nasty habit of making whatever they strike burst into flames. Understandably, thunderstorms in the high country are not to be taken lightly, and the absolute last place you want to meet one is on a mountain pass.

Another amazing attribute of thunderheads is how quickly they can form, and there are few things in life more unsettling than having one form right on top of you. From walking in the sunshine you can be facing torrential rain and lightning bolts in less than 10 minutes. Anyone with experience will tell you that, when it comes to thunderstorms and lightning in the high country, one quickly develops a deep appreciation for the subtle interplay between faith, hope, and destiny. Faith that the lightning will work the way it's supposed to, which is to say that it will generally strike the highest object in the area (which better not be you). A keen hope that destiny isn't holding anything against you, or, and this is *just* as important, that destiny isn't holding anything against the person standing next to you, because a lightning strike anywhere in your general vicinity is usually fatal.

Possessed with this knowledge and the knee-shaking fear that accompanies it, my desire has always been to keep as much distance between me and lightning as time and space will allow. Today I would soon be ready to run all the way back to Yosemite. We had been watching the sky since midmorning and were beginning to reconsider the wisdom of continuing our ascent. With storm clouds continuing to build rapidly, we stopped to discuss our alternatives and to get our rain gear out just in case, when the storm suddenly hit us with a vengeance. Immediately, rain started coming down in sheets, the wind began gusting to at least 30 mph, and lightning flashed overhead, followed almost immediately by a thunderclap, which meant that it was close, real close. No one needed coaxing at that point, and we achieved unanimous and unspoken agreement to march double time back down the way we had come, toward safety or at least something like it.

Below us about a mile from the summit we could see Warrior Lake, which comparatively speaking was rather sheltered from the storm. We soon arrived at a wide flat area just below and behind the lake, and, with the rain continuing to come down in buckets, pitched our tents in record time and jumped inside. The storm raged for another 30 minutes and then gradually subsided to a constant drizzle. Once again the boys were going crazy with boredom, and once again Susie was more than content to stay warm and dry inside our tent. Playing cards in the rain and the mud, however, wasn't appealing to anyone, so Steve and the boys and I all decided to try our luck at fishing.

We put our rain gear back on, retrieved our only fishing pole (which I had been carrying since Happy Isles) and as the rain continued to fall we headed to the lake. The first cast produced a fish and smiles all around, and over the next two hours we slowly walked around the lake, with each of us taking a turn with our lone "community" fishing pole. Once a fish was caught the pole was passed to the next person, who, after catching a fish, handed it to the next eager fisherman and so on. We kept a few to cook that night for dinner, and lost track of the number we caught and released after that. It was a GREAT afternoon — standing in the rain for hours with occasional thunder in the distance, sharing a single fishing pole between four guys, and all on a lake with fish literally jumping out of the water ...great memories!

The next morning dawned bright and clear and we reached Silver Pass at 10,895' well before noon. Once again the views were magnificent. Behind us on the horizon we could just make out Donahue Pass — that landmark at the boundary of Yosemite National Park, where seven days ago Susie and I had stood and looked out on the overwhelming vastness of what lay ahead. Now, looking back on that section of wilderness left me searching for words and meaning. The distance between the passes was about 50 miles. A span that millions of us routinely travel on the highway in less than an hour, had taken us seven *days*. Seven days, in which we had seen and felt, tasted, heard and smelled every foot of the land that lay between these peaks. It had left us not only with a deep appreciation of the vastness and beauty of the Sierras, but The Trail was also forcing us to experience and therefore see the world in ways we'd never imagined.

The ordinary things that had consumed so much of our everyday lives — paying bills, attending meetings, filling the car with gas — were not only unimportant on The Trail they had actually become *meaningless*. Life on The Trail meant that we were connected to our environment both literally and figuratively: where would we find water, could we make the next pass before the weather closed in, and so on. Fellow hikers (who by now had decreased to only a few per day) were not distractions or social obligations, they were people with stories to tell and often, having usually come from the south, valuable sources of trail information. Finally, there was a growing recognition of our dependence on one another, and the family and friends who had lined up to become sherpas for our numerous re-supplies. All of these conditions were aligning to force us out of comfort zones and paradigms we didn't even know we had and to examine our lives from a perspective entirely removed from civilization and all its conveniences.

Now don't get me wrong, for most of our entire journey I'd have killed for a fast car and a cheeseburger, but looking back across those mountains I couldn't help but reconsider my world view. By most standards I was well-read and well-traveled, but I was beginning to understand that I wasn't nearly as well-experienced as I had thought myself to be. With the occasional exception of carefully planned vacations, I had spent my entire life in the comfortable security of western civilization, but now I was immersed in a world and a lifestyle that was as far removed from my "real" world as it was possible to get without leaving the planet, and the juxtaposition of those two paradigms was as startling as it was unsettling.

It wasn't that I wanted to return to nature and become Rousseau's "Noble Savage" but, as I admired the view one last time and considered the experience it represented, I wondered if we don't sometimes pay a high price for our civilization and its conveniences. Our JMT adventure was bringing into sharp focus that, while the "real" world makes our lives easier to be sure, it also isolates us from one another and numbs us to our environment in ways so subtle and pervasive that it is often impossible to recognize.

Fresh fish for dinner! Our nephews Jake and Matt (left) helping Steve and me prepare a delicious meal at Warrior Lake.

Chapter 9

A return to Civilization

Leaving Silver Pass, The Trail descended steeply before entering a wide valley with a small, deep blue lake that was surrounded by low grass and patches of wildflowers. It's a lovely spot with a great view and, as I paused to admire the scene, I found myself thinking back to my first visit to this valley, when Steve and I had camped here so many years ago.

On that trip we had left early in the season when the snow was just beginning to melt in the higher elevations, and we'd had to battle for two days across snow fields and cornices with ice axes and crampons. We had finally arrived at this lake exhausted and cold just as the sun was beginning to set. With the wind howling and the temperature already in the 30's, I started to prepare dinner, while Steve tried to pitch the tent. With my back to him I heard the noise of our tent thrashing violently in the wind, and cries from Steve of "Auntie Em, Auntie Em!" I turned around at all the commotion and saw that the wind had caught our tent and turned it into a parachute. With both arms pulled over his head, Steve was barely hanging on, and both he and the tent looked like they were about to be blown straight up into the land of *Oz*. I ran over, and with our combined effort we just managed to hold onto the tent and get it deployed, but that first comical image of Steve, with both arms over his head, holding fiercely onto our fully inflated tent has always stayed with me.

This morning, however, it was warm with scattered clouds and downhill all the way to Lake Edison and I *mean* downhill. Plunging toward the bottom of the Mono Creek watershed, we began traversing countless switch backs, and soon gave up all the altitude we had gained yesterday and a little bit more. A few hours later The Trail finally leveled before proceeding straight up the opposite side over a series of switchbacks that were the mirror image of the ones we'd just descended, but that climb would mercifully be delayed. Instead we turned west onto a side trail that followed Mono Creek down to the lake and the ferry landing.

Lake Edison[8] is to hikers of the JMT what Hawaii must have been to those first sailors crossing the Pacific Ocean — an oasis in the middle of nowhere. This outpost in the Sierras is a remarkable enterprise that would warm the heart of any would-be entrepreneur. Known as Vermilion Valley Resort (VVR) and located deep in the mountains they are open, weather permitting, from June through October. Besides the foot traffic from the JMT, it can also be reached by car over a one-lane, bone jarring, cliff hanging, heart stopping, poorly maintained road that begins at Huntington Lake (which itself can only be reached from the Central Valley after a two-hour drive over a winding mountain road).

Despite its obvious location problems VVR caters to a wide variety of customers: backpackers, day hikers, boaters, campers, fishermen, hunters, and anybody else who happens to show up (including the occasional and very, very lost motorist). With this eclectic mix of customers, combined with a season that at best lasts only five months, the mountain resort operator must become all-things-to-all-people. Their offering therefore includes a: marina, campground, hotel, restaurant, bar, supermarket, sporting goods store, hardware store, laundromat, boat rentals, and the ferry service. Of

---

[8]Lake Edison is part of a hydroelectric project that was envisioned by an amazing engineer named John Eastman. In 1902 he had explored this section of the Sierras on horseback and sketched out a plan that would become "the hardest working water in the world." Initially completed in 1913 it remains an engineering marvel. Water stored at Lake Edison and nearby Florence Lake pass through a 13 mile tunnel of solid granite toward Huntington Lake, and eventually to the Central Valley. Besides producing hydroelectric power, the project also provides recreation on and around the numerous reservoirs, prevents flooding and provides irrigation water for Valley farmers through a maze of irrigation canals.

course all of these amenities have a certain mountain flair to them, but after almost two weeks on the JMT we thought we'd arrived at a Hilton Resort.

We began our "holiday" by boarding the ferry (a pontoon boat) for a ride down the length of Lake Edison to VVR. This is a beautiful boat ride under any circumstances, but is especially wonderful for backpackers because it saves a six-mile hike along the shoreline. Arriving at the marina (a sandy spot on the shore near the resort) I ran up the hill and managed to get the last two rooms: one for Susie and me, and one for Steve and the boys. I also received my very own VVR charge account — a secret code containing all the letters of my last name (actually, it *was* my last name). With it I could charge any of the myriad of services offered, which was good because <u>everything</u> was ala carte — right down to the towel. We checked into our rooms (a wood deck with a large canvas tent over it) and then walked over to the shower (a converted closet) where, for an extra charge, and for the second and last time on the JMT, we enjoyed a *hot* shower.

It was late afternoon by the time we all arrived back in our "rooms" and the weather, which had once again been building all day, cut loose. It was amazing! We had a commanding view across and down the length of Lake Edison, with Silver Pass in the background on our left and the unnamed mountain we would climb next on our right. The storm was centered between these peaks and lightning strikes peppered the area in between along with torrential rain. The rain and thunder were bad enough where we were, but we felt miserable for all the hikers still out in the high country tonight. We stayed safe and warm inside, but, with our "rooms" offering little in the way of amenities[9], we decided to head to the main lodge, where food, beer and entertainment awaited.

---

[9]Canvas tents aren't generally well-known for possessing a long list of extras and these didn't disappoint. Lacking running water and electricity, the only actual amenities in the room were four 3" mattresses, which smelled much like the old damp mattresses they were, which is to say they smelled *bad*. But it didn't matter - I knew that whatever odor they emitted would be easily overpowered by the smell of my own sleeping bag, and besides there would be two more inches of foam between me and the ground than what I was used to!

Fortuitously, we had arrived on Saturday night and that meant an all-you-can-eat BBQ along with a free beer to anyone hiking the JMT[10]. Walking past the bar (some plastic tables and chairs outside) we arrived at the Main Lodge. This was an old building, about the size of a double-car garage, and contained not only the main lobby, but also the restaurant, supermarket, sporting goods store, and hardware store. We entered and took the table next to the magnificent stone fireplace and ordered the special. The fact that the special was the *only* choice available didn't matter — we were out of the rain, the food was hot and tasty, there was a cold beer to go with it, and amazingly the Olympics were playing on a small T.V. in the corner. We were in backpacking heaven, and, between mouthfuls of BBQ, we passed the evening regaling each other and anyone else who would listen with tall tales of our adventures on the JMT.

All you can eat BBQ and a free beer at VVR.

The next morning saw us all back in the restaurant for "the mother of all breakfasts" — a cholesterol-fortified assortment of bacon, sausage, eggs,

---

[10]One of the greatest marketing strategies of all time. Throughout our entire journey every JMT hiker we met was aware that a free beer awaited them at VVR.

pancakes, toast, and coffee. We had just ordered when company arrived: our daughters, Amy and Bethany, as well as Steve's wife and son, Dorothy and Tom. They had all spent last night at Huntington Lake, and then caravanned the last leg of their drive early this morning. It was an exciting reunion and over breakfast we all listened as Jake and Matt, to the delight of their newly arrived audience, told story after story of their near-death experiences on The Trail.

It was the end of the journey for Steve and the boys, and shortly after breakfast they loaded their gear in the family car for the long drive back to Oregon. Susie and I gratefully accepted another re-supply box from Dorothy, and then it was time for good-byes. We promised to call in a couple of weeks (assuming we *survived* the next couple of weeks) and, even though Amy and Bethany were staying until early afternoon, Susie cried on cue when it came time to give hugs all around and wave good-bye as Steve, Dorothy, Jake, Tom and Matt drove away.

Susie and I had planned all along for today to be a layover day, giving us the opportunity to spend time with the girls and to rest up for the second half of our journey. So, with time to kill we decided to visit the Laundromat (an old washer and dryer hooked up to a generator and a propane tank on a flat spot of dirt near the "lodge"). The girls watched as Susie and I threw in everything we had except the shorts and T-shirts we were each wearing, and then we all headed back to our "room." The rest of the morning was spent re-packing — adding our newest re-supply and sending home extra clothes, a bathing suit, a small teapot, and anything else not deemed absolutely necessary for our survival.

Next, Bethany, who had been informed by her Aunt Dorothy (after she saw Susie and me in Red's Meadow) that we were both losing weight at a prodigious rate, produced an ice chest filled with assorted cheeses, power bars, sodas, two whole pies and some fresh fruit. It was overkill to be sure, but there was no denying that both of us (me especially) were looking rather skeletal, having each lost around 10 lbs in the last two weeks. So, I ended up adding the power bars and some cheese to our packs, ate two pieces of pie and promised to consume the fruit before we left.

By mid afternoon we had collected our laundry, enjoyed the lunch special at the restaurant, and settled our bill with VVR. It was time for the girls to leave. As we finished our hugs and good-byes, Susie went into maximum auto-cry, the girls weren't much better, and even my usual stoic reserve began to fail. I promised the girls once again to deliver their mother safe and sound at Whitney Portal, where, if all went well, we would arrive in two weeks at the end of our journey. With that assurance and a last round of hugs, Susie and I watched our daughters slowly drive away down the dirt road that would lead them back to civilization. We were alone again.

Virginia Lake on the way to Tully Hole. The two 1-liter water bottles in the foreground were gifts from our daughters, Amy and Bethany, and we carried them throughout the trip.

The ever changing
John Muir Trail

Above:
(Near Mather Pass)
*After Muir Pass most of The Trail
was a land of high alpine lakes,
towering peaks, and magnificent
granite basins.*

Left:
(Near Lake Edison)
*At times The Trail would plunge
into valleys of dense forests and
lush vegetation.*

Above:
Aptly named Cathedral
Peak in Yosemite
National Park

Left:
Amy, Hannah and Alisha
set up camp the first
night

Above: Susie takes a break from intermittent rain showers and writes in her journal. It rained some or most of everyday for 12 days straight!

Below: Donohue Pass. The horizon was more than 100 miles away, and we still had <u>twice</u> that far to go!

Chapter 10

Back into the abyss

I remember well my mood at that moment, and it wasn't good. I had just lost an argument with myself regarding my immediate future. Behind me on the road that had just carried the girls back to civilization lay warm beds, dry homes, and hot meals. Ahead of me lay wind swept Edison Lake surrounded by storm-infested mountains. Thunderheads stretched beyond sight in every direction, and the incessant rain was continuously punctuated by lightning. It looked like the Land of Mordor[11] and part of me could think of any number of reasons against reentering that cursed place. Indeed, after almost 100 miles and two weeks on The Trail, that same part of me was convinced that I had already experienced enough of Mother Nature for a lifetime.

It is at this point in our narrative that I should probably pause and attempt to explain something of the "me" and "I" so fondly referred to throughout this book. While it had always been normal (for me at least) to have occasional inner conversations—where would we go on vacation, which investment should we make, and so on—these generally resulted in amiable consensus. However, life on The Trail was stressing the various facets of my selfhood to levels never before experienced, and I was beginning to find myself being increasingly drawn into a conflict between three distinctly fractured and opposing camps:

- "Mr. Sensitive" who was completely into the experience—living in the moment and relishing the natural beauty of the Sierras.

---

[11]The evil empire of Sauron from J.R.R. Tolkien's <u>Lord of the Rings</u>.

- "Mr. Macho" who was absolutely dedicated to conquering the JMT and adding it to a list of other accomplishments.

- "Mr Civilization" who was a complete pain-in-the-butt and just wanted to go home and have a cup of tea.

Altogether it was to become a messy experience as these individual factions began to forcefully assert themselves and demand attention. In fact, well before the end of our journey, they became so unruly and argumentative that I would occasionally have to sit them all down, grab a long thin stick, and threaten the entire group with a lobotomy if they didn't behave.

But the full scop of these internal conflicts had yet to become apparent and, having just listened to the compelling wisdom of "Mr Civilization's" suggestion that a return to civilization was both necessary and prudent, I was rather startled by the sudden and assertive appearance of " Mr. Macho" who was gung-ho to continue. Throughout the day he had been offering several arguments for continuing the journey: the thrill of victory, the satisfaction of the quest, the sense of discovery. All had left "Mr. Civilization" unmoved until "Mr. Macho" (that bastard!) played the "Weenie Card" i.e., for the rest of your life everyone will know you are a "weenie" unless you do "X". The fact that "X" will result in great bodily harm or even certain death is seldom of any consequence. Given the choice—being a weenie or being dead—most guys (and I am a perfectly shallow example) will always choose the latter.

Knowing that further discussion with myself was useless, I decided on a subtle appeal to Susie's good senses and wondered aloud if maybe we shouldn't spend another night at safe, and mostly dry, VVR. No response. Whining proved equally ineffective, and, while I wasn't necessarily opposed to begging, I realized it would be futile. Susie had made up her mind: we were going back into the abyss. With the decision made, we once again put on our rain gear, lifted our packs and boarded the last ferry of the day back across lake Edison and into rainy darkness and despair. (Did I mention that I was in a bad mood?)

So it was that by late afternoon we found ourselves back in the wilderness on the eastern shore of Lake Edison (where we had boarded the ferry the day before). Under a light but steady rain, we picked up the side trail that led back to the JMT, and for the next hour or so followed its meandering course up Mono Creek. By early evening we crossed over Mono Creek on one of only a handful of bridges that exist on The Trail and set up camp near the base of our next ascent. Directly ahead of us was a series of endless switchbacks rising some 2,000 vertical feet, but they would have to wait until tomorrow.

Normally, we would have started hiking earlier in the day and continued longer, but the rain and thunderstorms were forcing us to alter our plans. In the High Sierras thunderstorm activity rarely starts before late morning, so for the rest of the trip we would carefully plan each major ascent to begin early in the morning. This new strategy would get us up and over the pass before lunch, and it was for this reason —positioning ourselves for an early morning ascent — that we made camp after hiking only a few miles.

The next morning therefore saw us up early and eager for our next climb. Actually, to be honest, eager may be a bit of an overstatement, and we *always* got up early anyway. The combination of light pouring in through the paper-thin walls of the tent, the sounds of various animal noises first thing in the morning, and the one-inch thick foam pad between us and the ground, all joined together each morning to produce a compelling get-out-of-bed experience that even Susie (who enjoys staying in bed more than anyone I know) couldn't ignore.

Just before we started I checked the map and looked up again at the mountain in front of us. I had traveled this next section of the JMT years earlier with two friends and a group of teenagers that included our daughters, Amy and Bethany. That group had come down this very section at the end of a grueling 15-mile day, and I remembered the switchbacks going on *forever*. So, I was somewhat apprehensive when we started out just after breakfast on the long climb up and out of Lake Edison.

As usual Susie slowly pulled ahead of me as we started up the swithchbacks. This continual and humiliating second-place position had by now become an almost daily experience, which I had at first tried blaming on all the extra community weight I was carrying. But the sad fact was that both of us were carrying almost exactly the same ratio of pack-to-body weight, at about 30%. I never could figure out how she hiked uphill so quickly, but I always suspected it was mostly to embarrass me. Strangely, however, going downhill was a different story altogether. Downhill was always difficult for Susie and the steeper the descent the slower she went. The basic problem was that, while Susie may have a long list of wonderful qualities, being nimble on her feet is <u>not</u> among them, and maneuvering down knee-high steps with a heavy pack had a tendency to move her center-of-gravity to places it had never been before. At first her sense of equilibrium tried to figure out these new coordinates, but it was never really able to rise to the occasion, and by now appeared to have given up the attempt entirely.

In spite of her balance-challenged condition, Susie was nothing if not determined and she would eventually plod her way down every mountain we climbed. More importantly her slow and careful navigation of every obstacle did prevent her from falling, even in some very difficult situations. But it was often a downright painful process to watch, and, honestly, every time we were on a long and steep downhill I thought I would die of old age.

Fortunately, today would be almost entirely uphill and I was greatly and pleasantly surprised when the two of us reached the top of the switchbacks by midmorning. Just over four miles and more than a 2,000 foot vertical gain in less than three hours was a pace we couldn't have imagined that first day out of Yosemite Valley. We were living the old cliché that "what doesn't kill you makes you stronger" and at the top of those switchbacks, as we looked back down on what we'd just climbed and checked it again against our map, we couldn't help but smile with the realization that we were in the best physical condition of our lives, and *maybe* we really could finish the JMT after all!

For the next day and a half we followed the JMT as it wandered

At just over 5' tall Susie often had to negotiate obstacles on The Trail that were almost as high as she was. Here a "step" is several inches above her knee.

through dense forest past the trail junction for Lake Italy[12], and then back up to Marie Lake, where we arrived just in time for lunch on the afternoon of our 15th day. At an elevation of 10,551' Marie Lake is a very large high-alpine lake, which sits in a bowl just below Seldon Pass. It is singularly beautiful and surrounded on all sides by magnificent peaks that rise to almost 12,000 feet. I had always wanted to visit this spot and, although I had once looked down on it from Seldon Pass, this was the first time I'd actually been there. Even better, I had very reliable information that the fishing would be great. So, it was with some enthusiasm that immediately

---

[12]This was the trail that the previously mentioned group had taken years earlier on a Trans-Sierra Trip, where, and to our great surprise and distress, we discovered most of the Lake Italy Trail had been abandoned years earlier. For more than two days our group had struggled over miles of snow fields, across acres of enormous boulders, and past huge sections of trail obliterated by recent avalanches. It was an adventure that was much more fun remembering than it was living thorough, and I was happy to walk quickly past that junction.

after lunch I got out my fishing pole (the one I had carried for more than 100 miles) and, while Susie sat contentedly reading her book, I walked over to the water's edge.

Anticipating my success I had the camera out and ready, and when the first cast produced an immediate strike I hollered at Susie to hurry over and take a picture. Unfortunately, I hadn't noticed that the memory card was full and Susie didn't know how to change it. Reluctantly I let the fish go, set the pole down and began rummaging through my pack looking for the spare memory card. To my surprise, while I was engrossed with the camera, I heard the unmistakable sound of my lure flying through the air and landing in the middle of the lake. Astonished (I didn't even know she could cast!), I turned around just in time to see Susie set the hook and smugly reel in her fish. It was a 10-inch Golden Trout — a huge fish for that species.

Trying (unsuccessfully) to catch another whopper at Marie Lake

I couldn't believe it! A hundred miles of carrying all that fishing gear and the minute I turned my back Susie sneaks away with my pole and catches a whopper. For the next hour I fished like mad, but the best I could achieve was a distant second place at eight inches. I'd been "hosed." Being out-fished by a girl was bad enough, but that stupid grin she gave me every time I looked at her was all but unbearable. Still, it was a nice long lunch break, and by early afternoon we reluctantly left beautiful Marie Lake behind, and headed up the switchbacks toward Seldon Pass.

We quickly reached the summit and stopped long enough to enjoy the views. They really were fabulous and as we began the descent down the other side we could see below us aptly named Heart Lake (it's shaped just like a giant Valentine's Day heart). Then it was on to Salley Keys Lakes, where we arrived late in the afternoon under cloudy skies and intermittent showers. We made camp and cleaned up next to a nearby stream, where our daily bathing routine from the freezing cold stream water was further enhanced by the freezing cold rain blown about by the freezing cold wind. We were both freezing shades of blue by the time we got back to our tent, where we put on all the clothes we had and tried to warm up. Finally, by early evening the rain stopped for the day, and just as we were walking down to the lake, the sun streamed through a break in the clouds and we caught the last rays of the day by the water's edge. It was another magnificent scene, and for almost half an hour we watched the twilight deepen, while the surface of the lake roiled with fish jumping up to catch their evening meal of assorted insects.

Chapter 11

We wait for the Hustons

The next morning we continued down The Trail toward Blaney Meadows, where we arrived about noon. Here we were to meet our friends, Mike and Paula Huston, who were bringing us our fourth re-supply of food and essentials. The only problem was that we had been hiking much faster than our original itinerary had foreseen, and the Hustons weren't due for another 24 hours. Months earlier, when we were in the planning stages of our JMT adventure, layover days had been discussed and abandoned as an unnecessary luxury, but now that one presented itself I was surprisingly frustrated by the delay. I was on a mission, I had a goal, and sitting still for a day wasn't on my to-do list.

Even so, we weren't going any further without more food; although, we did at least pick a pleasant spot to hold over. Leaving the JMT once again we took a side trail that led down to the South Fork of the San Joaquin River. On the other side of the river were excellent campsites, and, much more exciting, natural hot springs. Almost 20 years before, Susie and I, along with our daughters and another family, had arrived at this very same spot after hiking the six miles from Florence Lake. Here we had crossed the river and found the hot springs, where we soaked in its hot bubbly waste-high water, while the muddy bottom slowly but continuously oozed up between our toes. It was a combination of sensations that brought back vivid memories of delight in the warm relaxing water, and some considerable unease concerning what might lie at the bottom of that disgusting muddy pit.

But before we could relive any of those experiences we first had to get across the San Joaquin River, and we were having serious second thoughts because the water was running high and fast. After much discussion and considerable reconnoitering, we finally decided to give it a try. We removed our hiking boots, tied them to the back of our packs, put on our Tevas, and began to carefully wade across. Although a bit dicey, I reached the other side fairly quickly where I dropped my pack and started back across the river to help Susie. Seeing my approach she threatened me with one of her trekking poles, and insisted, with some authority that, "I can do it myself!"

I should mention here that Susie is a first-born child, which probably accounts for much of her stubbornness, as well as her general attitude toward authority and insistence on being in control at all times. I know this because I am a first-born child. So, I didn't take her refusal personally, but instead headed back to the shore to watch and wait.

I should also mention that trying to walk across large slippery rocks with freezing water rushing past was pushing Susie's previously mentioned problems with footing to the absolute limit. Bent over at the waist, and applying a death grip with each hand to a trekking pole, she slowly picked her way forward by carefully and deliberately moving one limb at a time. From my position on the far bank she looked like she was walking on four legs, and with her backpack now on top, one could easily imagine that she had suddenly morphed into some kind of giant turtle from the Jurassic Period.

By the time she reached the middle of the river I couldn't help but notice that the water was several inches deeper than the length of her lower leg, and the portion of her pants that she had carefully rolled up over her knee in order to keep dry was now completely under water. Fortunately, Susie was far too preoccupied with trying not to drown to notice. In the meantime, I had retrieved my lunch bag, and, while Susie provided the entertainment, I sat comfortably in the shade eating some jerky, trail mix, dried fruit, and had almost finished my Cliff Bar when she finally emerged on my side of the river shaken but triumphant.

After a brief rest we put our boots back on and headed for the hot springs, which we eventually found after exploring several false trails. It was just as I remembered it: about 10 feet in diameter and four feet deep, surrounded by trees on one side and bordered by a small meadow on the other. Even better, today it contained a rather attractive young lady, whose clothes, I couldn't help but notice, were all laying in a small pile next to her backpack.

Being the cosmopolitan guy that I am, I was willing to overlook this small breech of propriety and share the facility. Regrettably, Susie appeared to be of a different opinion. The furrow in her brow, the slightly upturned corner of one side of her mouth, the subtle shift of weight to one leg, and the way she kept hefting one of her trekking poles, all combined in an unmistakable body language statement of, "Not in your lifetime buddy!"

Sadly, we moved on from this beautiful spot and wandered further down the trail where we soon located the second feature of this natural water park. Tucked up against the mountain side and warmed by another hot spring was a small lakelet, and, though it was disappointingly free of the amenities we'd observed at our first stop, we were soon swimming in its warm and surprisingly clear water. There we spent a delightful afternoon floating in our little warm lake surrounded by nature's displays.

Behind us more than 3,000 vertical feet of granite rose up steeply from the back of the lake to become Ward Mountain, while on either side tall pines marched down the mountainside to meet the valley floor. In front of us a break in the trees revealed Blaney Meadows, and looking out across its acres of grass to the other side of the valley, we could see parts of The Trail as it snaked its way down the opposite mountainside, where earlier that morning we had descended from Salley Keys Lakes. It was an altogether perfect experience — floating in the midst of such loveliness — and we smiled through one last lap around the lake before we finally headed back to shore.

We found a grassy area near the water's edge, and lay there drying off in the warm sun. I knew we still had more than 100 miles and six major passes to go, but at that moment I was much more focused on the absolute beauty of our surroundings. It was almost overwhelming, and as I continued admiring the scene before us, I found myself remembering a much earlier trip with a similarly powerful experience.

It was a large group: three adults, eight teenagers, including our youngest daughter, Bethany; and we were on the third day of a trans-Sierra backpack trip. By mid-afternoon, Bethany and I found ourselves miles ahead of everybody hiking off-trail toward a distant snow-covered pass. Picking our way through the terrain we came upon a small lake shown only as a tiny blue dot on our map, but as we began the short descent down to the water, we both stopped to admire how astonishingly beautiful it was. Two small waterfalls emptied into the far side of the lake, while a narrow meandering stream provided an outlet on our side. The groupings of granite boulders placed about the lake's perimeter were everywhere accented by grass, small shrubs, and assorted wild flowers, while the entire picture was framed by spectacular granite mountains rising up to meet the impossibly deep blue sky.

Bethany and I must have spent 10 minutes just standing there commenting on the different aspects and qualities of our little lake, when for the first time it occurred to me that even if I had been given infinite resources to create a landscape as beautiful as the one before us, my best efforts would have fallen short. That in fact any attempt on my part to change or "improve" the current landscape would only serve to diminish it. It really was that perfect.

But even as I remembered that earlier adventure, and the extraordinary beauty of that little lake we had come upon, I could feel myself being pulled back into the present. The immediate beauty that surrounded us cried out for attention, and I was reminded once again how many times Nature provides us with perfection. It's right there in front of us whenever we sit beside a quiet meadow, watch a sunset, or hold a rose in our hand. It's a Truth that's easy to forget, but for most of that afternoon Susie and I remained at our little grassy spot by the lake enjoying the panorama before us as another perfect day drew to a close, and we finally left to set up camp for the night.

The next morning we awoke to find a big pile of fresh bear scat right in front of our tent[13]. Susie was a little unnerved, and we were both happy to leave the bear's territory immediately following an accelerated breakfast. We re-forded the San Joaquin River (it was just as exciting the second time) and hiked back to the junction of the JMT to await the Hustons.

With a couple of hours to go before their arrival, I emptied my pack and left Susie to guard everything, while I headed down the trail to meet our friends, who we hoped had managed to find their way to Florence Lake, had caught the morning ferry, and were even now hiking the six miles of trail toward us.

Sure enough, about an hour or so down the trail I saw two friendly faces making their way toward me. They were a sight for sore eyes, and what already appeared to be sore: feet, legs, and necks. It was this last part that particularly caught my attention. The plan was for Mike and Paula to not only bring us our much needed re-supply, but to also join us for the next two days as we made our way into Evolution Valley. Since this was Paula's first backpacking trip they (like all "first-timers") had apparently over-packed. The unhappy result was that they had run out of room in their own packs and had loaded our re-supply into canvas bags that hung loosely about their necks! They looked like a pair of pack animals with feed bags tied to their muzzles, and they must have felt that way, too.

It was hard to tell who was happier: me, knowing that our re-supply had arrived safely, or Mike and Paula, relieved that I was transferring those

---

[13]There's and old joke about bear scat (that's the technical name for poop). A Ranger is leading a nature hike in a forest heavily populated with bears. As a precaution all the participants are given small bells that tie to their shoes, and as the group walks through the forest there is a constant jingle from dozens of small bells. Presently they come upon two different piles of bear scat. Delighted the Ranger begins explaining that the first pile is from a Black Bear as he points out some remaining seeds and nuts that Black Bears typically eat. Next he points to the second pile of bear scat and declares solemnly that it is from a Grizzly Bear. "How can you tell?" asks one of the participants. "It has bells in it," replies the Ranger. ... Fortunately, the scat in front of our tent didn't contain any bells, but it was still pretty disturbing.

"feed bags" into my pack. Either way it was a pleasant reunion and together we hiked back to Susie's location, and more grateful hugs all around. The Hustons were eager to hear about our adventure, and we brought them up to date as we refilled our bear canisters and I reloaded my pack. It was at this wonderful moment that a portion of the mystery-of-the-full-packs was revealed to us, when Paula produced almost half of a fresh-baked apple pie that she had carried all morning.

While they politely declined, Susie and I each consumed a large portion of the most delicious apple pie I had ever eaten. Even better, when I tried to return what was left of the pie, Paula insisted that I finish it. Whether this was because she couldn't bear the thought of carrying it anymore, or (as both Mike and Paula would tell us later) she was frightened by how much weight I had lost didn't matter. It seemed that courtesy required me to eat the rest of it, and in a few happy mouthfuls I did.

Chapter 12

On to Evolution Valley

With our morning snack completed and all our packs ready to go, the four of us finally got back on The Trail and turned toward Evolution Valley. Because our friends had already walked six miles to get to us, and this was still their first day at altitude, we walked only a few more miles and stopped to camp for the night just as we entered Kings Canyon Park.

It was here, camped next to the Piuette River, that the final mystery-of-the-full-packs was revealed when Mike and Paula produced a <u>fresh</u> dinner of chicken and gravy with pasta, and most impressive of all: two cans of beer. It was the best meal I ever had, and Susie and I smiled all the way through it.

The next day we made great time and arrived at Evolution Valley under very cloudy skies by early afternoon. We got camp set up just in time to duck into our tents for the first of several brief afternoon showers, which would have been annoying if we all hadn't been so overwhelmed by our surroundings. Second only to Yosemite Valley in natural beauty and size, Evolution Valley lies at just over 10,000 feet and is surrounded by peaks rising to almost 14,000 feet. The south fork of the San Joaquin River wanders slowly down the middle and through three large meadows, any one of which deserved an afternoon's contemplation, but it was at the edge of the middle one — McClure Meadows — that we camped.

As soon as the rain stopped we moved our camp chairs and lunch next to the river. Here we spent the most pleasant afternoon of the entire trip watching the interplay of light, shadows, and clouds as afternoon thunderstorms swept across the imposing mountains surrounding the valley. Directly in front of us acres of meadow grass would suddenly burst into brilliant color as passing clouds parted momentarily to allow splashes of sunshine to leak through. If this wasn't enough, the entire performance was being replayed in the reflected waters of the river, which widened before us to become a glassy pond. We spent almost the entire afternoon mesmerized by the ever-changing beauty, and late in the day the last rays of sunlight managed to find a hole in the clouds. Suddenly, and for almost a minute, every peak was bathed in the red glow of sunset. It was a grand finale that brought spontaneous gasps from each of us and a mad dash for cameras.

Besides its remarkable beauty, Evolution Valley, which lies entirely within Kings Canyon National Park, also shares another similarity with Yosemite National Park; its fearless animal life. It was here that we had our most significant encounters with the fauna of the JMT. The first occurred about mid afternoon when Susie and I, trying to take advantage of a brief interlude of sunshine, were following a faint path down to the river's edge for a bath.

We had mostly disrobed and were walking barefoot through tall grass when Susie, who was in the lead, suddenly let out a bloodcurdling scream followed immediately by an astounding three-foot vertical leap to the top of a nearby boulder. For a moment I thought she must have been disemboweled and then flung aside by a Grizzly Bear and was relieved to discover that in fact she had only stepped on a four-foot long King Snake. I tried to assure Susie that "the snake was more frightened of her" but, frankly, neither of us believed it. In fact Susie might still be perched on top of that rock if only she had been more fully clothed, but in time her sense of modesty finally exceeded her fear of reptiles and we eventually made it to the river.

The rest of the day and evening passed pleasantly enough (including a second great dinner courtesy of the Hustons) until late that night, when another member of the Animal Kingdom decided to pay us a visit. With our bear canisters full from our re-supply, we had been forced to hang our trash from a nearby tree. Thinking back to our lectures from the Rangers at Yosemite, I assumed that any bear who could tell what was inside a tin can could surely tell the difference between trash and food, but we were soon to discover that Evolution Valley bears lack the olfactory discernment of their Yosemite cousins.

It was about 1 a.m. when I was awakened from a peaceful and comfortable slumber inside our tent to the sound of breaking branches and Susie's panicked whisper of, "What's that!"

Still trying to wake up I slowly replied, "Um... I think it's a squirrel knocking down pine cones" but even as I said it, we both heard the sounds of more and much bigger branches being snapped in two.

"That's <u>not</u> a squirrel, you idiot! There's a bear outside. Go out there and scare it away," Susie insisted.

"What?" I asked with growing awareness and rising panic, "Are you kidding me? I'm not going outside. It sounds like there's a bear out there!"

I felt momentarily better now that we were both clear on just who was doing what, but just as quickly realized we still had a problem — outside in the dark there was a huge beast with big claws and even bigger teeth, who was looking for something, or perhaps *someone* to eat. I began a quick inventory of our options and wondered momentarily what macho thing Captain Kirk of the Starship Enterprise would do. Shoot first with full phasers is what he'd do, but at the moment I couldn't even produce a sling shot. The transporter! I remembered. I'll transport the bear to another location. Better yet I'll transport *me* to another location. Home would be good!

It was a great idea, but, even at that moment, seemed to lack a certain practicality. So, I was just beginning to consider if either John Wayne or McGuiver might have any insights, when I was startled out of this useless exercise and back into reality by the sound of more breaking branches. The bear, which had begun his visit by being merely ravenously hungry, had at this point achieved a level of frustration only experienced by ravenously hungry bears who have just discovered they are trying to eat a bag full of empty foil wrappers and plastic bags.

By now my anxiety was rising at least as quickly as the bear's frustration and had begun strongly manifesting itself as a little inside voice that was wondering if now wouldn't be a good time to find a "happy place" and go there. Suddenly, I felt years of conditioning from early childhood welling up inside me. This was the conditioning that said, "whenever there's a monster outside, the safest place to be is under the covers with a flashlight." Finally, I'd hit on a plan! Quickly reaching for my headlamp, I turned it on and there we both were: inside the tent, crouched within our sleeping bags, and looking at one another with just the sort of expression one has whenever one is pondering the question of who is going to be eaten first.

It was pathetic, really. We both knew that the tent couldn't protect us against anything more aggressive than mosquitoes, but still, especially with the headlamp on and bundled inside our sleeping bags it gave the comforting illusion of safety. Besides I could tell that as we lay there Susie was attempting to employ her Jedi mind-powers of persuasion on the bear, and was telepathically communicating: "There's nothing in the tent. You don't need to go there."

So, with nothing between us and the bear except our paper-thin tent and the "power of the force" we waited for the bear's next move. Fortunately, anti-climatically, and to our everlasting relief, the bear discovered his mistake and left in disgust as quickly as he'd arrived. I waited a while longer and finally found enough courage to poke my head outside. Peering into the dark I could just make out Mike Huston's head emerging just as cautiously from their tent. Finally, convinced that the bear had really left, both of us boldly emerged to inspect the damage.

Sure enough, in the beam of our flashlights, we could see that the garbage had been tossed almost everywhere, and the trash bag looked like it had suffered almost as much injury as our male egos, which is to say that it was mostly shredded. It took us a while to clean up the mess, but we were soon able to return to our tents and confidently assure our wives that the garbage itself had survived pretty much undamaged, and that we had successfully frightened the bear away. Neither of them believed the last bit, but to their credit they were both polite enough not to point and laugh.

Evolution Valley at sunset

Chapter 13

We almost die, again

The next morning, after our usual breakfast of oatmeal and tea, it was time to say good-bye. Mike and Paula were turning back toward Florence Lake, and Susie and I needed to reach Muir Pass by early afternoon. We exchanged hugs and promises of safe journeys with the Hustons, while Susie cried as quietly as possible. It had been a memorable and enjoyable few days with our friends, and we were both sad to leave them behind.

Departing Evolution Valley, we began a gradual ascent toward our next pass. The miles passed by quickly and by mid afternoon we had arrived at Wanda Lake. Sitting a few hundred feet below Muir Pass, Wanda Lake, which was named for one of John Muir's daughters, sits near the middle of a large open plateau at 11,500 feet. It is surrounded on three sides by high mountains with a broad opening on the north end, which leads back down to Evolution Valley. It is starkly beautiful, and, it would soon turn out, just the type of place that trail guides refer to when they caution against staying in exposed areas that are subject to high winds. (This overlooked fact would later explain why it was that we were the *only* people staying within five miles of this particular spot.)

The weather had been particularly unsettled all day, but for once had turned calm and warm while we bathed by the edge of the lake. In fact it was too hot for Susie to read inside the tent and she soon joined me outside, where we sat in our chairs and watched a series of thunderheads begin to stack up above the mountain tops that surrounded us. Despite our immediate shirtsleeve micro climate, we soon realized that the weather was about to turn very bad, very fast. Indeed we were moments from discovering that we had managed to select a campsite location that would become the Sierra Nevada equivalent of the eye of a hurricane.

With the weather quickly deteriorating, we re-secured the tent with heavy rocks to hold down all the stakes and then dug a small trench around it to divert any rain water away. Next, after removing enough food for dinner and a minimum amount of kitchen necessities, we covered our packs and stacked rocks on top of them so they wouldn't blow away. It was looking nastier by the minute and Susie ducked into the tent, while I stayed outside to cook the quickest one-pot-meal we had. By now the weather was really closing in. Black clouds covered the sky, the wind kicked up and in moments was blowing 30 to 40 mph, while lightning began to strike the mountain tops only half a mile away. I decided dinner was as ready as it was ever going to get, and after putting another big rock on top of the stove, carried the entire pot into our tent just as hail began to pelt the area.

The next few minutes were to become some of the most memorable of our lives. As we sat inside our little tent, the hail started coming down in shovelfuls and the temperature plummeted almost 50 degrees to below freezing. For the moment we put dinner aside and instead began putting on all the clothes we had, and then wrapped our sleeping bags around our legs for added warmth. Outside the storm was getting worse. The thunder and lightning were stupendous and by now almost continuous. Worse yet, the time delay between the lightning flash and the sound from the thunderclap was becoming so short that it was almost simultaneous, which meant that the lightning strikes were getting closer, <u>much</u> closer. With no place to run or hide we took the only precaution we could, which was to fold our therm-a-rest pads in two, thereby doubling their thickness and insulating ability, sit cross-legged on top of them, and hope for the best.

By now the wind had increased to well over 40 mph, which was whipping up tsunami-like waves on Wanda Lake and sending them crashing on the shore just 100-feet away. As they smacked against the rocks the wind carried the water spray along with the still-falling hail, which all began hitting us squarely on Susie's side of the tent. I looked over and there she was: her shoulder leaning into the wall of the tent and one arm outstretched in a valiant attempt to keep the wall from collapsing. It was crazy! For awhile I thought we had wandered onto the movie set of <u>The</u> <u>Perfect Storm</u> and it looked like we both going down with the ship.

With Susie still providing our last line of defense against the elements there was nothing left for me to do but wait. Well, actually, there was dinner, and in the midst of these many and continuous near-death experiences I decided there was no reason to die hungry. So, I reached for our rapidly cooling one-pot meal and started shoveling it down. Wordlessly, Susie had arrived at the same decision and managed to turn around, prop the tent against her back, and, while the storm continued to rage outside, we passed the dinner pot back and forth.

Much later, from the safety of civilization and the distance of time, I would look back at this experience as being one of the defining moments of the entire trip. As might be expected, there is generally a rather memorable quality to surviving any near-death experience (and this one was about as near as it could get). But there is a more angst-filled reason that this event has stayed with me.

I have always found the high country of the Sierra Nevada to be a spiritual place. There among the isolation and beauty of the mountains I have often encountered a deep sense of peace and connectedness — a "presence" to which I had come to associate not only power but also the added qualities of awareness and benevolence.

The issue therefore was that as we sat huddled in our tent that night with the storm raging around us, wondering if the next lightning strike was going to turn us into charcoal, I began to suspect that there might be something seriously wrong with my cosmological interpretations. In the midst of the explosions of lightning, the wind tearing at our tent and the waves crashing on the nearby shore, there was no denying that power was a correct and unmistakable attribute of the mountain gods, but I was having a great deal of trouble trying to resolve the whole awareness and benevolence thing. Based on the evidence, I could see only two possible alternatives: either the power was benevolent but lacked an awareness of our existence, or we had offended it in some way and it was actively trying to kill us.

At that moment the evidence strongly suggested the latter, and we were both as surprised as we were relieved that in the end it didn't succeed, but the alternative — benevolence without awareness — was deeply troubling. Perhaps I had missed the point entirely by trying to assign human attributes to otherworldly powers, or (and I fear this is the more likely) by assuming that my existence was of any real importance to the Universe in the first place. Whatever the correct answer, it was certainly disappointing to learn just how much work my spiritual paradigm still needed.

With that transcendental question still hanging in the air (as it were) the storm raged on for amost 30 minutes and then suddenly ended. Slowly we emerged from our tent in just the same fashion as I'd always imagined Noah and his wife emerging from the Ark, which is to say very timidly and with a large helping of humility. We could see the last of the thunderstorm as it raced southward beyond Muir Pass, while to the northwest the remaining clouds were quickly breaking up.

We were alive! And, we both looked at each other with smiles of biblical proportions as we stood huddled together outside our tent. All around us we could see the yellow rays of the setting sun burst through the clearing sky in what had only minutes before been a life-threatening environment. Peace and tranquility had returned to the High Country as quickly as it had left, and we watched in utter amazement as the warm glow of sunset light played across the mountain tops and the clouds of the departing storm, even as the entire light show was being reflected back by the now calm waters of Wanda Lake.

It was another surreal experience and when I finally climbed into my sleeping bag that night, I found myself more metaphysically confused than I had ever been in my life. The Universe had thrown me another curve ball and I was reluctantly adding another "swing and a miss" to my scorecard. I laid there for some time trying to sort out the whole attributes-of-the-Universe problem, and wondered, just as I fell asleep, if I shouldn't just settle for "magnificent capriciousness" and leave it at that.

Our tent at Wanda Lake after the thunderstorm suddenly ended

Chapter 14

Susie clears everything up

The next morning we trudged on toward Muir Pass. We couldn't know it yet, but the weather had finally changed. It would remain unsettled and almost constantly threatening for another few days, but Wanda Lake proved to be the last time we encountered rain. It became a great, great relief to both of us — the end of spending part of every day being wet and cold, and, more wonderful still, the end of trying not to become human lightning rods every afternoon. Additionally, we would soon discover an unexpected consequence of all the terrible weather we had endured these last 12 days — more than 90% of the JMT hikers had left The Trail. For the rest of our trip (until Mt. Whitney) we saw only a handful of fellow backpackers.

We reached the summit of Muir Pass at 11,955' by mid morning where we stopped to admire the view and the small stone hut built by the Sierra Club in honor of John Muir himself. It is a beautiful and much-photographed spot, and almost everyone hiking this portion of the JMT pauses to enjoy the setting and to spend a few moments resting inside. Here one can easily imagine spending the night in its large single room warmed by the giant fireplace that dominates the entire south wall. Of course, this fantasy requires that you: first, don't mind sleeping in a rock building that is frequently struck by lightning; second, are willing to fight off the resident marmots, who seemed entirely convinced that they owned the place; and third, that eight miles ago you had the foresight to collect firewood, because that's where the last trees lived. (Indeed we hadn't seen even a blade of grass in almost two miles.)

Still it was a nice if not altogether practical gesture on the part of the Sierra Club, and I was trying hard to remember that it was the "thought that counts" in spite of my rapidly deteriorating mood. The basic problem was that I had been here twice before, and while it is an undeniably beautiful spot, it also marks the beginning of the descent into Le Conte Canyon. I *hate* the descent into Le Conte Canyon. It's endless. Dropping almost a vertical mile it descends, often steeply, as it methodically follows the middle fork of the King's River for more than 10 miles. Then it finally levels out, for about the length of a football field, before turning abruptly east and straight up a grueling 10 mile ascent to Mather Pass, where if all went well we would arrive three days later — right back at our current altitude.

It was an absolutely depressing idea, and we sat there for some time as I looked at the map, reread our trail guide, looked back at the scenery and then started over. It didn't make any difference. No matter how much I stared at the map, how many times I read the trail guide, or how closely I examined our surroundings two glaring facts kept coming back: 1) we were going straight *down* for 10 miles; 2) we were going straight back *up* for another 10 miles — end of story.

Actually, it almost *was* the end of the story. I was already having a really bad morning and looking down into Le Conte Canyon wasn't making it any better. Down, down, down we went, and The Trail got worse with every step. As bad as last night's storm had been at Wanda Lake, it had hit much harder on this side of Muir Pass, and we walked through and around several sections of washed out trial and the remains of numerous campsites destroyed by last night's torrential downpours.

After 20 days in the wilderness, I was beginning to seriously question what I was doing on this godforsaken hike. By now we had endured everything the JMT and Mother Nature could throw at us: 12 straight days of rain, bears, lightning, blisters, and enough freeze-dried food to change anybody's outlook on life. And here we were this morning, with death and destruction in our wake, walking blithely *toward* the storm that had just tried to kill us last night.

It was at this point in the trip (as I was going down, down, down, both literally and metaphorically) that "Mr. Civilization" put the finishing touches on a plan for escape that he had been working on since ...well, since the day after we left Yosemite Valley. It was a simple plan, but it required a certain amount of stealth and cunning to execute properly. But with 120 miles of motivating trail behind me, along with five major passes and Mt. Whitney in front of me, "Mr. Civilization" felt we were up to the task.

"You know," I began casually to Susie, "we don't have to finish The Trail." With no response whatsoever I waited for what seemed like the correct and casual amount of time before adding, "I mean if <u>you're</u> not having a good time we could take the next side trail and be out of the mountains by tomorrow." Still no response, and I could feel the momentum beginning to slip away. This one-sided conversation wasn't going nearly as well as "Mr Civilization" had promised, but I pushed on anyway, and, while I strove valiantly for a tone of indifference, I'm afraid that instead I achieved what could only be described as an air of desperation when I added, "Not that we'd go home right away. After we got off The Trail we could hang out ...and go shopping ...or something."

Believe me when I tell you that as bad as it sounds now, it was much worse if you had to be there. "What!" I thought to myself, "go shopping? ...go shopping!" "You IDIOT!" What happened to stealth and cunning? Susie's never going to buy that drivel, and of course she didn't.

Pausing briefly for effect she stopped in the middle of the trail, turned around slowly and looked me in the eye. "Listen" she said, "if <u>you</u> want to leave The Trail that's OK with me, but you're not blaming this on me. I'm still ready to finish."

I tried to recover with, "No, no, I don't want to quit. I just thought that if you weren't having a good time I'd be willing to leave The Trail ...for your sake."

It was awful, and my pathetically transparent attempt at recovery seemed to hang in the air embarrassed by its very existence. Mercifully, and to her everlasting credit, Susie let it go and we simply walked on. It was the turning point of the trip for me: I realized for the first time that, short of a broken leg, Susie wasn't going to quit and there was no way I could live with the idea of being beaten by a "girl." The Trail was probably going to kill me, but I knew at that moment that the only way I was getting off the JMT was either in a body bag, or hiking out through Whitney Portal — nine days and almost 100 miles away.

Chapter 15

Mather Pass and the staircase from hell

By late afternoon we were nearing the bottom of miserable Le Conte Canyon when our route intersected the side trail that lead over Bishop Pass and out to the South Lake trailhead. Always before I had followed that trail, but today we passed it by and entered, what was for me, new territory[14]. This last 90-mile section of the JMT is the most inaccessible, the least traveled, and, we were about to discover, by far the most difficult of the entire trip. Soon we would discover that the first 120+ miles of the JMT were mostly a warm-up for this final obstacle course, and to our utter dismay find ourselves agreeing with that first ultralight backpacker we had met so long ago outside of Red's Meadow. The one who casually opined that the first 60 miles out of Yosemite Valley was the "easy" portion of The Trail.

Over the next nine days we would seldom be below 10,000 feet and, of the seven major passes on the entire JMT, five were still in front of us. Worse yet, one of those passes was over 13,000 feet! The reader may wish to linger over that last sentence, because in my mind a 13,000 foot *pass* is an oxymoron. A pass is something you cross to *avoid* mountain peaks, but, for reasons known only to the original (and I was beginning to suspect, sadistic) planners of the JMT, we seemed embarked on a journey whose primary purpose was to *find* mountain peaks.

---

[14]In the preceding almost 20 years I had traversed nearly half of the JMT on various backpacking trips, but had never seen the approximately 40 miles between Cathedral Peak and Reds Meadow, five miles on the north side of Seldon Pass, and the final 80 miles between the bottom of despicable Le Conte Canyon and Mt. Whitney.

But I'm getting ahead of myself, and I should stop here and confess that, while hardships awaited us, so too did landscapes of unparalleled beauty. We were entering a land almost entirely above tree line, a land of granite, shaped everywhere by ancient and now long departed glaciers. It was here that we would find much of what the JMT is so famous for: high alpine lakes, towering peaks, and magnificent granite basins. Here we would find views that were as stark as they were beautiful, and that every day left one searching for words...

By late morning of the next day we had reached the base of *The Golden Staircase*. This is a much-talked-about section of the JMT, and for the last several days almost every hiker coming from the south had warned us about it. Despite its poetically inviting name, we would soon decide that a more appropriate and certainly more descriptively accurate name would have been *The Vertical Ascent of Infinite Steps*. It begins as a series of steep switchbacks that soon turn into rough granite steps ranging from 8" to 24" high. Our guide book mentioned that this was the last section of the JMT to be completed, and it's easy to see why. Built on the sheer rock face of the gorge of Palisade Creek it proved to be the most arduous ascent of the entire trip, and one can only imagine what it must have been like for the poor trail crews who constructed it. It took most of a very long afternoon climbing the "staircase" before we finally reached Palisades Lakes at 10,613', and while the views below us and of the knifed shaped peaks rising behind the lakes were certainly spectacular, neither of us found them nearly as memorable as the climb itself.

It was late afternoon before we arrived at a large bench[15] a few hundred feet above the lakes and here we set up camp among the boulders and a few stunted Lodgepole Pines. From here we had a commanding view of the entire basin, which looked like an enormous granite temple. About two miles to the south we could see Mather Pass, a small 12,100' notch in the mostly 14,000 foot mountains surrounding us, while a hundred yards behind us a waterfall fed the stream that ran calmly and briefly across our

---

[15]A mostly level area on the side of a mountain. This particular bench was the size of several football fields.

bench before cascading down to the lakes below. All in all it was as spectacular a view as anything the Sierras had to offer

Still admiring our surroundings, I remember how unimpressed I was as I began matching up the various landmarks around us to the place-names on our map. It was as though the U.S. Forest Service, having finally arrived at this last section of The Trail, found that all but one of the names they had allocated to the entire project had been used up. Thus it was that behind us stood Palisades Peaks, which fed Palisades Lakes below, whose outlet, Palisades Creek, flowed down into Palisades Canyon. Don't get me wrong— I like *palisades* as much as the next guy — but four times in one basin seemed to indicate a certain lack of imagination.

Despite this oversight of nomenclature, it was perhaps our prettiest campsite of the entire trip. Better still, we had the place to ourselves. After a quick bath we did some laundry and jumped into our fleece pants and jackets before hanging our wet clothes on a line to dry. Next we splurged by cooking the only extra food we had — dehydrated peaches that we turned into a cobbler and enjoyed with hot tea. It was the best afternoon snack we'd ever eaten, and both of us savored every bite as we watched the sun slowly set on the multiple and resplendent palisades.

As soon as the sun disappeared the temperature started to plunge and we quickly fixed dinner — a typical assortment of re-hydrated: top ramen, pasta with meat sauce, and corn. Compared to the cobbler it was mostly tasteless (frankly, it was mostly tasteless compared to unleavened bread), but still it was warm and filling, and, with night closing in we put on an extra layer of fleece, climbed into our sleeping bags early, and slept peacefully until morning.

We awoke to a stiff wind blowing down from the snow-covered peaks above us. It was the coldest morning so far and it took awhile before I reluctantly emerged from the tent and ran over to the clothes line to retrieve our laundry from last night. It was here that I made the unhappy discovery that our clothes, while not exactly wet weren't exactly dry either. They were frozen stiff! Susie's predictable response to this news was to burrow deeper into her sleeping bag, and it was some time before I could coax her out.

I finally got the stove to boil enough water for our morning tea and

Making cobbler below Mather Pass. The temperature plunged into the 20's that night and the clothes we had hung out to dry all froze.

instant oatmeal[16] and thus fortified, we eventually broke camp and began the hike toward Mather Pass. The Trail stayed in the freezing shadow of Palisades Peaks all morning until we arrived at the top of Mather Pass about 11 a.m., where we found sunshine and more spectacular views.

Mather Pass is near the center of Kings Canyon National Park, and its summit provides a 360-degree panorama of some of the most awesome granite on earth. Standing there, we both kept turning in slow circles

---

[16]The fuel canisters we carried for our stove used a propane mixture that didn't work well in temperatures below thirty degrees Fahrenheit, and we wouldn't see morning temperatures above freezing for the rest of the trip. I tried to get Susie to put one of the canisters in her sleeping bag at night so it would be nice and warm in the morning, but the idea never really caught on.

trying to take it all in. At just over 12,000 feet we had reached our highest elevation so far, and in every direction we looked, as far as we could see, granite peaks knifed 13,000 feet to 14,000 feet into the sky. However, after carefully checking our position against the map, what really brought a respectful smile to our faces was the discovery that the *lowest* point in our entire viewshed — for as far as we could see in any direction — was an astonishing 10,795 feet. There was no doubt about it; we really were in "The High Country."

We both wanted to stay longer, but, as beautiful as it all was, the icy winds howling through the notch of Mather Pass wouldn't allow it. Even with our coats on we were starting to shiver, and we had to get out of the wind. Mercifully, as soon as we started down, the wind stopped altogether and the heat of the sun and its reflection off the granite switchbacks we were descending soon began to thaw us and our still-frozen laundry from last night (which we had tied to the back of our packs).

The rest of the day was the best hiking of the entire trip. It was warm, it was flat (relatively speaking), and there wasn't a cloud in the sky. It was that last part that I particularly remember. As the reader has no doubt surmised, the last 150+ miles had been stressful for any number of reasons, but the unrelenting rain, and, most especially, the daily afternoon lightning storms, had been downright oppressive. It wasn't that either of us had a lightning phobia *per se*, it's just that we were fairly certain being hit by over a million volts of electricity would prove to be mostly terminal. Now, after almost two weeks of being chased by the lightning gods, two weeks of wondering, "is this the day I'm going to be smote?" we were both relieved beyond description that it was over.

As we walked on, enjoying both the scenery and the wonderful change in the weather, I kept coming back to my almost giddy reaction to blue skies. Why was I suddenly so happy? The answer was, that like almost everyone living in 21st Century Western Civilization, I had taken basic shelter for granted. But not any more, and as I continued pondering the ramifications of my new awareness, I found myself thinking hard about Thoreau and the ideas he expressed in his famous book, Walden.

I had read the book years and years ago and had promptly filed its central idea of living very, very, simply, under "lifestyles to be avoided." Today, however, I wasn't so sure, and with my new attitude I began thinking of Thoreau's simple cabin on Walden Pond and the conversation I might have had with a rather confused real estate agent:

Me:	"OK, you've got a single-room cottage with a fireplace, two secondhand windows and a door."
R.E. Agent:	"Yes, that's about it."
Me:	"It sounds GREAT!"
R.E. Agent:	"It does? But the place doesn't even have electricity or running water"
Me:	"So? ...It's got a roof doesn't it?"
R.E. Agent:	"Well, of course"
Me:	"And it's *never* been struck by lightning?"
R.E. Agent:	"What? No ...we don't really get much in the way of lightning around here."
Me:	"Oh, that's *perfect*! When can I move in?"

Looking back I still find this episode one of the most memorable of our entire journey, and a powerful affirmation that how we view our lives is less a matter of circumstance than it is of perspective. In other words, how one *feels* about life depends almost entirely on how one *looks* at life. It's a truth I often forget, but on that day I found myself walking through the wilderness as happy and content as I have ever been in my entire life. Why? Because for the first time in weeks I was warm and dry, and, with nothing but blue sky, there wasn't a chance I was going to be struck by lightning. That's why!

Chapter 16

We find the "real" Rangers

We reached Marjorie Lake (11,132') by early afternoon and there we met the only Forest Ranger we would see on The Trail. In fact, we met two: Trapper and Roxanne, a husband and wife team whose assignment for the summer was to patrol the back country of Kings Canyon National Park. Here, finally, were the "rugged, and fearless individual ready for adventure" that I had looked for and failed to find in Yosemite. These two were the "real thing" and Susie and I listened in awe as first Trapper and later Roxanne told us a little about themselves.

Two years earlier they had completed the Pacific Crest Tail (PCT) — a 2,650 mile long trek from Mexico to Canada — of which the JMT composed only a small portion. By itself this was an absolutely unbelievable accomplishment (and I was already wondering if they might be from the planet Krypton) but it got better. For the last two summers they had *requested* their current assignment, which was to live in a tent about a mile north of us and just off the JMT. From there they would spend days at a time on solo trips searching this remote section of the Sierras for trail problems and hikers in distress.

It was an inspiring story, but what really got my attention was how it related to our own situation. Until this chance encounter I was sure that over the last 22 days Susie and I had, on occasions too numerous to recount, endured the "worst of all possible worlds," but here was living proof that I was *wrong*. It could be much, much worse! You could be stuck out here for *months*. Worse yet, just as we neared the 200-mile mark on our own JMT adventure (and the pleasant self-righteousness that went with that milestone) Trapper's and Roxanne's example revealed just how low we were in the hierarchy of backpacking accomplishment. Defying all common sense and decency, here was a couple who had hiked <u>ten times</u> further than we would.

Despite this humbling comparison with the "residents" of Marjorie Lake, we still counted this stop as among our favorites. We'd hardly seen anyone in days so Trapper and Roxanne were a reassuring presence. Nicer still was how excited they were for us. Our own JMT adventure had brought back great memories for them of their PCT hike, and it was immensely reassuring for Susie and me to listen to some of their stories and their ready admission of how difficult life on The Trail had sometimes been for them.

Besides the pleasant company and reassuring stories, before they left, Trapper and Roxanne also showed us the "secret" campsite, and we counted it as among the best of our entire trip. Hidden behind some rocks and small trees, it looked out on a 10-mile-long granite masterpiece of a valley that bore the distinctive "U" shape caused by the scouring of glaciers over eons of time. If possible our view was even better than the one we had enjoyed earlier from atop Mather Pass, whose distinctive notch we could still see on our northern horizon. Turning to the south we could see sections of The Trail as it skirted Marjorie Lake before beginning the predictable switchbacks up to Pinchot Pass on the horizon. It was an inspiring panorama and we both agreed that if you had to spend an entire summer in the Sierras, it couldn't get much better than this.

We sat outside and continued to admire our surroundings over an early and leisurely dinner, but soon the sun began to disappear from the faces of the tall peaks that dotted our skyline. We really wanted to stay out longer, but at 11,000 feet temperatures drop quickly after sunset, and we were soon forced to beat a hasty retreat to the warmth of our tent and sleeping bags.

Once inside the tent we both turned our headlamps on and began what had, for the last couple of weeks, become our nightly maintenance and repair routine. Out came the first-aid kit and we went to work on our numerous and assorted blisters, cuts and contusions. Our feet were the first order of business — I was still plagued with heel blisters from Red's Meadow, and Susie was struggling with multiple blisters on her toes and the loss of two toenails. But despite these problems and the other multiple cuts and minor infections we each had, our biggest concern was becoming our continued weight loss.

Each of us had lost about 10 percent of our body weight, and while Susie was certainly looking thin, I had begun to resemble a walking skeleton. By now I had lost almost 15 pounds and was still losing about half a pound per day. The previous week, when my pack had quit fitting, I had begun wrapping my fleece pants around my waist. This added enough girth to my middle to be able to tighten the hip belt on my pack and put some much-needed padding on my hip bones, which were sticking out rather conspicuously. Now my collar bones were starting to chafe and for the rest of the trip I would "wear" my extra socks under my shoulder straps in an attempt to prevent shoulder blisters. It was getting serious. I had never been this thin in my adult life, and I knew that in another day or two I would start losing muscle mass.

The fundamental problem was that our carefully chosen and prepared backpack food just didn't have enough fat in it, and both of us were simply burning more calories than we were eating — a lot more. Worse yet, since leaving the Hustons in Evolution Valley, we had been on the longest and toughest section of our entire adventure, and we had eaten far more food than I had planned for. This meant that we would be mostly out of food by tomorrow, and our next re-supply wasn't scheduled to arrive until the day after that at Woods Creek Junction. With this rather serious problem upper most on our minds, we broke camp the next morning and headed up toward Pinchot Pass.

Chapter 17

Food, wonderful food, glorious food –Oliver

As usual Susie slowly pulled ahead of me as we started up the switchbacks to Pinchot Pass. Although it was probably the easiest pass we encountered because the ascent was so gradual, it was still freezing cold that morning and walking uphill at 12,000 feet is a chore no matter how shallow the incline. Still bundled up in my fleece jacket I could see Susie about a quarter mile ahead and gaining on me as I methodically placed one foot in front of the other and followed the switchbacks up, up, up. I had stopped briefly at one of the turns to catch my breath when I noticed something wonderful a few feet off The Trail. Two grouse[17] were nestled among the rocks. Their splotchy coloring exactly matched the surrounding granite and I would never have noticed them if I hadn't stopped at this exact spot.

Normally I would have admired their markings, or the social behavior that had paired them together, or even wondered at their migratory habits, but not this morning. Today all I saw was lunch! Still wearing my pack and standing perfectly still I began to discuss with myself the delicious possibilities. I would fry them up with some oil and serve them with wild rice. Oops, we didn't have any oil or rice. Hell, we didn't even have a frying pan anymore. OK, no problem, I'll barbecue them. Idiot! There's no wood; we haven't even seen a tree for three days. Relax, I told myself, we'll just boil the damn things. Hey, it's not elegant, but it'll get the job done.

Now, all I had to do was get them into the pot. Let's see, I've got a spork and some duct tape. I could tape the spork to a long straight shaft of wood

---

[17]Grouse are game birds about half the size of a chicken and very tasty.

and make a spear. What? Oh yeah, we don't have any wood. OK, I'll get a cardboard box and a stick and some string then build a trap like I did when I was six years old. Huh? I don't have any of that stuff either? Well fine, how about I just hit them over the head with a big rock? Now we're talking. I'll hit both of them simultaneously with a rock and boil them right here on The Trail. I like it! Simple and to the point.

I am sorry to report that it was at exactly this point in our narrative, just as I was starting to ever so slowly drop my pack, that the fatal flaw in my luncheon strategy was exposed when both birds simultaneously flew away. Whether their departure was due to some telepathic ability on their part or because they had noticed my excessive drooling I was never quite sure, but I can tell you it was heartbreaking knowing that they wouldn't be joining us for lunch.

About an hour later I finally caught up with Susie at the top of Pinchot Pass, where I found her waiting comfortably on a flat rock that overlooked the Woods Creek watershed and our next destination. The wind was calm, the sun warm, and we sat there quietly eating an early and unhurried lunch as we admired the view, especially the way the sunlight was being reflected off the many tiny lakes dotting the landscape below. Ordinarily this would have been the highlight of the day, but all I could think about was our dwindling food supply, and as I stoically ate the very last of my trail mix I kept imagining how delicious boiled bird would have been.

We stayed a bit longer and just after noon, with only a single Cliff Bar between us to share before dinner, we started back down The Trail heading southward once again. It was another steep descent (second only to dreaded Le Conte Canyon), and we were soon following Woods Creek as it plunged more than 4,000 vertical feet through towering canyons on its winding way toward Cedar Grove Trail Junction. Our plan was to arrive there the following day by mid morning, but this section proved more inhospitable than we had anticipated and all the campsites were either terrible or completely nonexistent. We therefore found ourselves putting in another very long day before finally arriving at the junction by early evening.

We crossed over a narrow suspension bridge, aptly named *The Golden Gate of the Sierras*[18], to reach the east side of Woods Creek, where we found several developed and unoccupied campsites. It was a nice spot, but we'd have to wait until tomorrow to appreciate it. Tonight we were tired, sore, and hungry, and it was well past dark by the time we finally got dinner ready.

The main entree that night was Spam, and, while this is a food item that is generally scorned in polite society, I can even now remember how delicious it was that evening. This fact alone should give one a fairly accurate sense of just how hungry we both were, and how serious our food supply had become. We always carried some extra food, but because this leg of the journey had been so strenuous we'd eaten it early on, which meant that we'd been on short rations for the last couple of days. In fact, when we got into our sleeping bags that night, the *only* food we had left was two packets of instant oatmeal, a few tea bags, and one package of top ramen. If our re-supply failed to arrive tomorrow, we were in trouble.

The next morning after a meager breakfast we started to do some serious waiting. If everything went as planned, our good friend, Bill Shearer, would arrive around noon with our final re-supply, but it had been more than a week since we'd had any communication with the outside world and any number of problems could have arisen. I figured I could hold out until lunch before I started to eat the bark off the trees, but by dinnertime lone hikers would be in danger.

---

[18]On the JMT almost all stream and river crossings are get-your-feet-and-legs-wet experiences; however, there are a handful of crossings where the water runs deep and fast and bridges have been erected. They are almost all simple metal truss bridges that are as sturdy as they are uninspiring. But the bridge that stood before us was different. It was a suspension bridge built entirely of wood and steel cables, which had been carried in by mule and horseback. It was nearly as beautiful and impressive as its namesake, and much more of a thrill to cross! Its capacity was one hiker at a time. This was because after advancing just a few steps onto the narrow two-foot wide walkway the entire suspension bridge began to move freely both up and down and from side to side, and one had to hang on tightly to the thin steel waist-high cables that provided the only handholds.

With nothing to do I wandered around our immediate area exploring the suspension bridge once again, walking down to Woods Creek and finally ending up at a nearby campsite where a family from British Columbia was staying. They too had arrived last night, having hiked up from the Cedar Grove Trailhead two days earlier. As I spoke with the parents they explained they were planning a five-day hike through the Rae Lakes area and then back out to Cedar Grove. They were having a great time but complained that their three teenage children weren't eating nearly as much as anticipated and they had way too much food to carry.

What a bummer, I thought to myself, I've started to hallucinate. Apparently, our food shortage was even worse than I had feared. However, I wasn't about to take any chances and decided to play along just in case. As an added precaution, remembering my sorry bird experience from the day before, I tried not to drool either. We continued talking, and to my very great relief, the two of them didn't dematerialize the way mirages are want to do, nor did they run away in fear. So, as casually as I was able to manage, I suggested that if there was *any* food they didn't really want I was ready to do the right thing and help solve their problem.

So it was that by mid morning I returned to our camp with a swagger in my step, and, with my best attempt at a heroic flourish, produced a few pounds of Canadian trail food. Susie immediately wanted to know if there was an unsuspecting hiker buried nearby in a shallow grave, but I assured her that we were in fact only helping our fellow and less-fortunate backpackers. I fired up our little stove and in a few minutes we were eating delicious hot oatmeal fortified with milk powder, brown sugar, protein powder, and dried fruit. It was a superb breakfast and while we sat in the sun, on a log near our "kitchen," we smiled at every comforting mouthful and at what a wonderful morning it had turned out to be after all.

Things got even better when, just before noon, Bill and his friend Paul arrived right on schedule. They had hiked a day and a half to reach us, and, while I was genuinely pleased to see them both, I must confess that the full measure of my heartfelt gratitude was mostly directed at the re-supply they were carrying. We were SAVED! In fact we were better than saved because not only did they have our scheduled re-supply, but they had brought extra food besides. Weeks earlier Bill had promised to wait for two days at this junction if Susie and I were late, which meant that he was carrying at least an extra day's worth of food, and, just like our new best friends from Canada, Bill couldn't want all that extra weight.

For the second time that morning I was looking at a win-win situation that politicians and professional negotiators only dream about: Bill didn't want to carry all that extra food for another 20 miles, and I didn't want him to either. So, with Susie's occasional help, I began to whittle down the extra crackers and cheese, the extra trail mix and dried fruit, along with anything and everything else Bill would relinquish. I ate two lunches, snacked until mid afternoon, had another lunch, and continued snacking until early evening when Bill announced that appetizers were ready.

I should mention here that Bill considers himself quite the gourmet backpacking cook, and especially prides himself on his presentation. Susie and I wouldn't disagree on either count. For the first course, he and Paul had packed in a fresh cheese tort and some French bread along with a pint of wine. More astonishingly, in honor of my birthday, which was a few days away, Bill also produced a small blowup birthday cake and birthday cards from our daughters. Caught momentarily off guard, Susie went into auto-cry, but recovered quickly and we all began to enjoy the hors d'oeuvres. The wine didn't go far between the four of us, but it was quite the treat, and we saved a few sips to go with our second course, a meal-from-the-gods of fresh chicken Cordon Bleu and wild rice. It was fantastic, and after we'd enjoyed everything and really couldn't eat another bite, Bill and Paul served a dessert of cookies and fresh coffee. The meal was to-die-for, and to say that Susie and I were impressed or that we enjoyed the dinner party utterly fails to convey the mood of the evening. Perhaps, if you combined the feeling one gets after any near death experience along with the childlike joy of your first trip to Disneyland, you'd be close. They're both impossible to adequately describe, but the result is that you find yourself smiling at the whole world because every sense is heightened and everything seems extraordinary.

In short it was a perfect evening, shared with good friends, good food, and all under a starry sky, surrounded by every beauty the High Sierras can offer. When I finally waddled into my sleeping bag that night it was with a renewed sense of awe and a contentment known only to those fortunate few, who have consumed more than 12,000 calories in seven hours without puking. How I managed the last part I can't say, but I awoke the next morning feeling better than I had on the entire trip.

Above: Paula Huston and Susie near Evolution Valley. The sign on the bridge under construction (which they had just crossed) read: "Unsafe, do NOT cross!" After all we had endured and were about to endure this feeble attempt at ensuring our safety seemed a bit absurd.

Below: Our water bottles on Mather Pass looking toward The Palisades

Inside the tent at Wanda Lake. Sitting on our Therm-a-Rest pads while thunder and lightning raged outside, we wondered if this was our "last supper."

Right.
The "Golden Gate" of the Sierras. This beautiful suspension bridge could accommodate only one hiker at a time.

Above
Cascade Valley on the way
to Lake Edison.

Left
Susie catches "my" fish at
Marie Lake.

Above: Riding the ferry across Lake Edison, where family, food, shelter and a <u>free</u> beer awaited us.

Below: The view from Seldon Pass

Chapter 18

What do you mean this isn't Glen Pass?

Surprisingly, Susie skipped most of her normal meltdown routine when it was time to say good-bye to Bill and Paul the next morning. At first I was puzzled at this behavior, but eventually determined that this unexpected change was due not to any lack of affection toward our stalwart friends, but rather to Susie's evolving and increasing comfort with living in the mountains. (More on this in a moment.)

I, on the other hand, had a very special place in my heart for these guys, which I reserve for anyone who has just saved my life by hiking uphill for almost two days with 20 wonderful pounds of food and supplies, and I came dangerously close to having my eyes leak. It was a near thing and I barely managed to get by with a firm handshake, a slap on the shoulder, and a heartfelt "thank you" to both of them. With that our respective groups turned in opposite directions and headed out: Bill and Paul directly west and back toward civilization, while Susie and I headed southeast toward Rae Lakes.

The rest of the morning went by quickly as we climbed steadily upward past Dollar and Arrowhead Lakes. Soon we spotted Fin Dome, a dramatic and easily identifiable granite column, which rises almost 1,000 feet above its surroundings, and just before noon we arrived at beautiful Rae Lakes, almost two hours ahead of schedule. (It was amazing what a full day of rest and thousands and thousands of calories can do.)

We stopped for lunch at a lovely spot overlooking the lake and within a stone's throw of a great campsite Bill had recommended to us earlier. It was here, as we sat comfortably enjoying ourselves and discussing our afternoon plans, that I was reminded yet again that Susie and I... how shall I say this... sometimes experience life a little differently.

As near as I can tell she pretty much ascribes to the old cliché, "life is a journey, enjoy the ride" and incredibly, despite all that we had endured in the last three weeks on The Trail, Susie found herself growing ever more comfortable and enjoying her "ride" on the JMT. Lamentably, my comfort pendulum was swinging in exactly the opposite direction. Intellectually I understood the wisdom of the journey analogy, but my own nature is just a bit more goal-oriented, and, while the whole adventure was undeniably extraordinary on any number of levels, after 25 days on The Trail I was about "journeyed" to death. Moreover, "Mr. Civilization" had by now become convinced that there is just so much beauty a guy can take, and we'd passed that point somewhere around Seldon Pass. Indeed, in the last few days his overall view on the subject was becoming ever more narrow, and was in fact beginning to achieve a clarity and focus seldom experienced by mortal men — *We had to get off this Trail!*

Looking back it might have been this ever-growing sense of purpose that may have contributed to my possible overreaction when Susie suggested that we set up camp for the night, "What?" I replied. "Are you kidding me? We've only been hiking for three hours! It's not even noon yet! We took yesterday off! We..."

I was still getting warmed up when Susie, who must have suspected just how much more whining lay ahead, cut the exchange short by saying, "Of course you're right, dear. I don't know what I was thinking. Let's put our packs back on and hop over this next 12,000 foot pass before dinner."

OK, so maybe that isn't exactly what she said, and maybe she didn't talk to me for the next two hours, and maybe by mid afternoon, when we were still struggling up the almost vertical face of Glen Pass, I was wishing Susie had been a little less understanding and that we had in fact stayed at Rae Lakes, but what really made this such a special day was that by late afternoon, when we finally came around that last bend in the trail, the one where we expected to see the summit about 50 yards ahead, it wasn't there!!!

We had crested a false summit and what had been hidden the entire afternoon now loomed before us. Here was the *real* Glen Pass about a quarter of a mile ahead and more than 1,000 feet straight up! I must say that, while I found this sudden turn of events completely unpleasant, Susie was positively apoplectic about it, and it looked like ol' Mike was in for another and much longer installment of the silent treatment. Which, with so little to lose, is why I felt emboldened enough to take out the camera and ask Susie to stand still and give me a snarly look, while immediately replying to my own rhetorical question with, "Oh, never mind. I see now that you already *have* that look."

Not surprisingly, this witty remark had the effect of ending all verbal conversation for the rest of the afternoon, and we instead began communicating in body language, which for Susie consisted of a single hand gesture. I responded with my best attempt at a forlorn and pleading shrug, and the "conversation" ended. With that we both sat down to consider our options, which for Susie, I found out later, included justifiable homicide. After a quick survey of our surroundings and a fresh look at the map, we both saw that there really were only two possibilities: go back down toward Rae Lakes where we last saw water and a flat spot to camp, or get over Glen Pass before dark. They were both unpleasant choices and Susie, who was by now fully entrenched in "silent mode," signaled her decision when she wordlessly got up, grabbed her pack and began marching up the pass.

The rest of the afternoon was mostly miserable as we slowly zigzagged up a relentless series of very steep switchbacks. Finally, at about six that evening we reached the summit at 11,978'. To our astonishment we arrived just as three different groups of hikers converged on the same spot. This was more people than we'd seen in a week, and reassuring evidence that the weather was clear to the south of us. We lingered on top for a few minutes and briefly exchanged stories and trail tips with the different groups, but with darkness fast approaching Susie and I were soon back on The Trail as we headed down the south side of Glen Pass.

From the summit the JMT drops very steeply and in less than a mile we arrived at the base of the switchbacks, where we found a small lakelet and a very tiny flat spot (though not particularly level) just big enough for our tent. We skipped our normal bathing routine that night and both settled for a quick swipe with a wet towel. By then it was nearly dark and we barely had enough energy left to cook dinner by the light of our headlamps before we both dove into our sleeping bags and fell instantly asleep.

1,000 feet below its summit, Susie gazes silently up at Glen Pass and considers her options.

Chapter 19

Forester Pass

We awoke to another cold morning, and, although Susie was still a bit subdued in her excitement at being on this side of Glen Pass, she was at least talking to me by now, and I could tell that, secretly, she was almost as happy as I was to have that "butt kicker" of a pass behind us. At least I was pretty sure she was happy about it. Besides, this morning our attention was mostly riveted on what lay about 15 miles in front of us — 13,180' Forester Pass. A 13,000 foot pass! What were they *thinking*? Didn't these "trail-builder-guys" ever consider going *around* the mountains?

Next to Mt. Whitney, Forester Pass was by far the highest point on The Trail, and Susie and I had worried about this monster ever since we first saw it in our trail guide months ago. It was this concern coupled with yesterday's unpleasant encounter with Glen Pass that prompted the two of us, before we ever left the relative warmth of our tent, to engage in some lengthy discussion about just when, where, and how far we were going today. We eventually decided to hike about 12 miles, camp just below Forester Pass, and then attack the summit the following morning.

It was still early morning when we headed down The Trail, with the temperature just below freezing and our jackets zipped right up to our necks. In spite of the cold it was a beautiful morning, and within a couple of miles the temperature had warmed enough to produce another pleasant and cloudless day in the mountains. Even better, with the exception of a single hiker that morning, we had the place to ourselves, and we didn't see another soul until late the following day.

We made a gradual 1,500 foot descent into lovely Vidette Meadows where we turned southeast to intersect Bubbs Creek and began following it on a long and generally moderate 2,500 foot climb toward Forester Pass. Just a few weeks ago hiking 12 miles at this elevation with a 4,000 foot up and down differential would have been impossible for either of us, but, after almost a month of daily conditioning, neither of us thought much about it, and by mid afternoon we had arrived in high spirits at our destination: an unnamed lake just below Forester Pass.

Our plan was to camp here, but we were beginning to second-guess ourselves as we surveyed the unexpected starkness of the landscape. In fact, with the single exception of our small lake, it looked like we had landed on the moon, and at just over 12,000 feet we thought we nearly had. At this altitude, which would be our highest campsite of the entire trip, stark doesn't begin to describe the terrain. There were no trees, no shrubs, no grass, not even a bug. I mean this place was so barren it didn't even have dirt! Nothing but rocks for as far as you could see (and from 12,000 feet you can see pretty far!)

Searching among all those rocks we finally found a decent campsite, where rain and snow runoff had deposited enough decomposed granite to form a flat spot large enough to accommodate our tent. It was as barren as the rest of the landscape, but it did offer some protection from the wind, which was to prove surprisingly important later that night. Best of all, it had a nice view of our little lake with mighty Forester Pass in the background.

By the time we got camp set up it was still early afternoon, which gave us enough time to bathe, do all our laundry, and still have time for tea and cookies before dinner. Tragically, the cookies turned out to *be* a tragedy. Months before, during all our preparations, I had experimented and failed numerous times with different cookie recipes but eventually produced a fried cookie of which I was inordinately proud. To the dry ingredients I added some maple syrup and margarine, then formed the dough into thin squares and placed them on a hot frying pan. The result would never be mistaken for anything my Mom used to make, but when you're backpacking a hot, sweet, cookie-tasting piece of anything is pretty delicious, and I had made these earlier on The Trail with great success. Unfortunately, through a mix-up, our last re-supply didn't contain any margarine, we were out of maple syrup, and the fry pan had been sent home two weeks ago to save weight.

Undaunted by these issues I skipped the maple syrup altogether, ingeniously substituted olive oil for margarine and dumped the resulting goo into one of our pots. In moments I had balls of hot goo that smelled a bit like pizza, stuck to the pan like super-glue, and had the look and texture of something that had already been eaten once before. In a word they were frightful, but the really sad part was that we ate every bite. They tasted almost as bad as one would imagine, but they were loaded with calories. More importantly, they didn't taste *anything* like dehydrated food, and, if you swallowed them quickly and washed them down with hot tea, one could almost imagine they were good.

So there we were alone in the high country, sitting comfortably in our backpack chairs and slowly enjoying our tea and "cookies." With our front row seats it was a perfect afternoon, and I still remember trying to absorb the magnificence of our surroundings. The granite "temple" in front of us surpassed in beauty and sacredness every religious monument I had ever visited: cathedrals, shrines, monasteries — nothing manmade came close. Everywhere were rocks and impossibly high mountain peaks whose stark outlines and monochromatic brown tones were made all the more beautiful by occasional splashes and broad brush strokes of vivid colors. In front of us our little lake calmly reflected the deep, deep blue of the sky, while off to one side our laundry, hanging between two rocks on a clothesline, fluttered on a soft breeze and provided startling shapes of primary reds and greens. The mountains themselves seemed to reach into space and the unearthly contrast between them and the intense dark-blue violet of the sky was a treat available to any who are lucky enough to venture this close to the heavens.

To my mind this was the essence of what life on The Trail was all

Below Forester Pass — our highest campsite at 12,000 feet.

about. It was life unfiltered. It was life in the first-person. In the *Everyday World*, equipped with satellite radios, blue tooth cell phones, and an almost infinite choice of CDs, most of us drive to work each morning with no awareness of our journey ...and we think this is *normal*. On The Trail these kinds of disconnects are not possible. You <u>see</u> the panoramas at every stop, <u>smell</u> the butterscotch scent of every nearby Jeffrey Pine, <u>taste</u> the cold and refreshing water you just pumped from a mountain stream, <u>feel</u> the ground with every step, and <u>hear</u> the wind in the trees. On The Trail life is an in-your-face experience. You cannot be a disinterested observer looking at life through a window or living it vicariously through a television.

Earlier I speculated that life on The Trail was a daily lesson in the Yin and Yang of existence, and here, just below Forester Pass, school was in session. It wasn't that this landscape was any more beautiful than countless others I had seen in the Sierras (and the few that I have previously tried to describe). Indeed, its absolute lack of any discernible life would have caused some to label this entire area as a barren wasteland. But by now I knew better. Rather than waterfalls or meadows, the astounding beauty that surrounded us lay in the incredible contrast between earth and sky, just as the power of the Sierras lay in the contrast between the serenity of this moment, and the violence of the thunderstorm we had encountered at Muir Pass. Altogether it produced a sublime experience that was felt as much as seen, and for just a moment I wondered if I had glimpsed the absolutes of beauty and serenity that philosophers and mystics, had for millennia, tried so hard to describe. For me it may have been the best moment of the entire trip.

But nothing lasts for long in the mountains and by about 5 p.m., when the sun dropped below the peaks that encircled us, it was as if the mountain gods, having provided such an ideal afternoon, suddenly remembered that to keep everything in balance, we would need to get "Yanged" before dinner. This time they decided to send wind, and, from being absolutely calm all day, a breeze began to blow the moment the sun set. It continued to get stronger and we re-secured the tent and stacked extra rocks on top of our packs and other gear just to be safe. Meanwhile the wind had reached the howling stage and we beat another hasty retreat into the tent where we ate dinner and bundled up against the cold, which by now had dropped to below freezing. The wind storm lasted all night, and, with the noise from the constant fluttering of our tent along with the bitter cold, neither of us got much sleep.

Happily the wind finally stopped just before daylight and after another early breakfast we started up The Trail on a very cold but otherwise beautiful morning. From here it was only two really long switchbacks followed by a few short ones near the top of Forester Pass, and by 10 a.m. we were at the summit, where we stopped for a long break. The view was nice, but we were far more excited to just *be* there. We had dreaded this pass the entire trip, but, perhaps because of the way we had staged it, or that it was such a gradual incline, or maybe because we had "psyched" ourselves up for it, whatever the reason, we would both remember it as one of the easiest passes of the entire journey.

I would also remember Forester Pass because today was my 52nd birthday, and, while I've never considered birthdays all that important, there's a contemplative part of me that has always looked forward to birthdays as a time to reflect, and this morning "Mr. Civilization" was reflecting on what the hell I was doing at 13,180' and why was I still wandering in the wilderness after 27 days? "Mr. Civilization" didn't know, but he was astonishingly clear in terms of an action plan: *We had to get off this Trail!* His ingenious plan envisioned us abandoning our packs right here, then simply *running* the last 40 miles to the end of The Trail, where I was sure to find a cheeseburger, a beer, and all the other trappings of civilized society.

Fortunately for all of us, Susie, who never seemed to have much trouble with schizophrenia, chose this very moment to bring the entire group back into focus by presenting me with a birthday card that she had been carrying for 187 miles. This was exactly the kind of strange, yet strangely predictable behavior that, over the last 35+ years, I had come to expect from her. For weeks now I had been cutting the strings off the tea bags in order to save weight, even while she had been carrying this card for almost a month. I knew that if conditions had been reversed and I had somehow thought to bring a card for her birthday (remember this is strictly hypothetical) I'd have pulled it out at our first stop in Tuolumne Meadows, shown it to Susie so she could memorize the verse for later, and thrown it away. So, despite the card's somewhat travel-worn appearance and the strange incongruity of holding a greeting card on top of Forester Pass, I found myself reading it with enthusiasm, and smiling at Susie's thoughtfulness and the sheer weirdness of the morning.

Chapter 20

Susie clears everything up ...again

The drop down from Forester Pass was just that: a 2,000 foot plus fall down the steepest switchbacks we had seen on the entire trail (worse even than The Golden Staircase) and Susie was unable to negotiate many of the steps without help. (At just over five-feet tall herself some of those steps almost reached her waist!) It was a brutal decent and we didn't reach the base until afternoon.

Way behind schedule (mine not Susie's), we stopped for an abbreviated lunch before getting back on The Trail, and for the next few hours hiked across a high barren plateau with no redeeming qualities that either of us noted. In fact, it was easily the most nondescript portion of the entire JMT, but by mid afternoon the mountain range on our left side ended abruptly and suddenly we could see all the way to the eastern side of the Sierras. There in the distance, not more than ten miles as the crow flies, stood Mt. Whitney!

Overjoyed doesn't begin to express my feelings. We had been looking for this stupid mountain for almost 200 miles and finally there it was before us. It was the *best* mountain I had ever seen! We stopped just long enough for pictures and then hurried along. It was getting late and we still had a few miles between us and Wallace Creek, where good campsites and a particularly beautiful stream awaited us.

We arrived by early evening and both of us were beat. It had been a long hard day and, though Susie was pleased to see Mt. Whitney, she would have been perfectly content to have stopped hours earlier and saved the view for tomorrow. I on the other hand was ecstatic. When we got in our tent that night I couldn't wait to get out the map and study our progress.

Our map was actually a series of 13 individual maps, which showed the JMT beginning in Yosemite Valley on plate #13. From there each successive map detailed a different section of the JMT as it wound its way southward finally arriving at Mt. Whitney on plate #1. Throughout the journey we were constantly looking at the appropriate map to measure our progress, and plan where to stop for lunch, refill water bottles during the day, and camp each night; and, of course, to make sure we didn't get lost. Sometimes we could walk across an entire map in a single day, but then there were other times when The Trail would seem to lose track of itself and begin a circuitous route through the entire quadrant. On the worst of these we could sometimes linger for three or four days unwillingly exploring every mountain and valley on the entire map. But, whatever the circumstances, it was always a cause for celebration to retire one map and move onto the next.

So, what made today so extra special was that not only had we succeeded in our protracted search for Mt. Whitney, but a few hours ago we had finally walked onto map #1. It was the *best* map we were ever "on." We'd been looking forward to this milestone since leaving the parking lot in Yosemite Valley, and now for the first time the end of our trip was in sight (or at least it was on the map). It was a wonderful feeling and I went to sleep that night secure and content in the knowledge that only 22 miles lay between me and salvation.

The next morning I woke up and I *had* to get off The Trail. I had dreamed about it all night and was now willing to admit that "Mr. Civilization's" previous idea of running the last 40 miles was perhaps a bit extreme, but today a simple 22-mile hike seemed imminently doable, because I *had* to get off this trail. I knew I had to get off this trail. I had been saying it for days and the closer we got to the end of The Trail the stronger the urge to finish became. Susie, on the other hand, was going "native" on me, and the longer we stayed out, the more comfortable she seemed to be with the whole experience. The differences in our "realities" could hardly have been more extreme, and I tried to convey this to Susie in a story my father always used to tell: the Parable of the Salmon and the Trout.

A trout lives in a large deep pool in the river. Every spring he watches in disbelief as one salmon after another swims past him and up the churning cascade of water that empties into the pool he calls home.

Salmon:	*(resting briefly before the next leg of his journey)*
Trout:	"Hey, bud where ya' goin?"
Salmon:	"Who me? I *have* to get upstream."
Trout:	"Why? What's the hurry? Why not stay here and enjoy the moment?"
Salmon:	"I can't stay <u>here</u>. I *have* to get up stream."
Trout:	"Don't you realize that once you get <u>there</u> it will become another <u>here</u>? And then you'll just want to go to some other <u>there</u>, which will then become <u>here</u> all over again."
Salmon:	"Don't give me that Zen crap! I know the difference between <u>here</u> and <u>there</u> and let me tell you 'bud' the difference is that <u>here</u> is fresh out of cheeseburgers and beer!"

All right, the truth is my Dad never told me a parable in his life, but the story clearly illustrates why salmon have always been revered as the wisest creature in the animal kingdom, or were they the most obsessive? I can't remember, but the point is that no matter how I looked at it or tried to calm myself down and be in the "now" all I could think about was the fact that we only had 22 miles to go and I wanted to be *DONE!*

So, before we left camp that morning Susie and I ended up having, what in diplomatic circles is generally and politely referred to as, "a frank and open exchange of ideas," concerning just how much longer we would be on the JMT. It turned out that my new plan for a 22-mile death march was as much of a nonstarter for Susie as my previous idea of running the last 40 miles. However, her idea that we spend a leisurely few days slowly wandering toward the finish line was so awful that I threatened to disembowel myself. Finally, we compromised on a two-point plan: A) we'd be out in three days or less; and B) I <u>had</u> to quit whining.

It was part 'B' that probably saved my life. In the past couple of days I had become insufferable, and when moments ago I had threatened ritual suicide, Susie had immediately offered helpful suggestions on how that might be accomplished. Consequently, when we finally resumed our journey that morning it was with a certain amount of apprehension on both sides. Susie wasn't entirely convinced that I still wouldn't just drop my pack and start running toward Whitney Portal screaming "I have to get off this Trail!" and, for safety purposes, I was keeping an increased distance between the two of us least she sneak up and hit me over the head with a big rock. But, even if we weren't yet holding hands and singing "Kumbaya" together, we were at least mostly back on the same page in terms of expectations, and the two of us headed into the last section of The Trail with a renewed commitment that one way or another we'd finish this thing together.

Chapter 21

Mt. Whitney at last!

We reached Crabtree Meadows by noon and suddenly there were hikers everywhere. During the summer months the U.S. Forest Service allots 160 permits each day for hikers on the 11-mile trek from Whitney Portal (our final destination) to Mt. Whitney. Because of the trail's popularity there is a lottery system for permits, and every day there are scores of disappointed hikers. However, for those determined enough, there is an alternate and much longer route around the back side of Mt. Whitney, and it was these unlucky yet resolute hikers that we were beginning to encounter. After days of almost complete solitude it was unnerving to be around dozens of people, and it was about to get downright crowded.

Even though we had only hiked about six miles, our plan was to stay at Guitar Lake, which was the last major stopping point this side of Mt. Whitney. I was still ready to hike all night and finish this thing before morning, but had to agree that trying to tackle the grueling ascent of Mt. Whitney this late in the day probably wasn't a good idea. To our surprise the only decent campsites at Guitar Lake were already taken by large groups, and the few remaining lousy sites were full as well. Our trail guide promised even poorer choices further up, but we decided to give it a try anyway. Fortunately, and, for the first time, the guide was incorrect and about ½ a mile later we found one of our favorite campsites of the entire trip tucked behind a small hill just off The Trail.

We pitched the tent and by mid afternoon we were sitting on our "front lawn" in our camp chairs enjoying the view. It was awesome! Two ponds lay directly in front of us and behind them a small meadow opened up to provide an unobstructed view of the backside of Mt. Whitney. It was a visual wonderland all by itself, but was made even more extraordinary by the pulsing activity that occurred throughout a long afternoon.

At the far end of the meadow a small section of The Trail was visible and we watched scores of hikers march past. There were couples, and groups, and occasional individuals. They were old and young, colorful, drab, slow, and fast. They were the robust, and they were the walking wounded, limping with blisters and strained muscles. It was a constant parade of humanity, and we literally saw more people that afternoon than we'd seen the previous three weeks.

As interesting as the people-watching was, it paled in comparison to the most unexpected and incongruent event of our entire trip — fighter jets. East of Mt. Whitney lies the Owens Valley, which opens into the Mojave Desert. There the Air Force and Navy both have large training bases, and apparently Mt. Whitney, being the highest point around, marks a heavily traveled leg of their practice area. No sooner had we sat down expecting to enjoy the beauty and serenity of our surroundings, when two jets burst over Mt. Whitney right on top of us! They were loud, they were fast, they were low, and we were both so startled we nearly soiled ourselves.

Just over 20 jets buzzed Mt. Whitney that afternoon. Some in formations, but mostly in ones and twos, and every time it was astonishing. Then around 4 p.m. they all went home and were replaced by two hang gliders soaring peaceful and quietly at about 15,000 feet as they slowly circled the mountain. Finally, as evening approached, all human evidence disappeared from the sky as huge clouds began to form, and shadows from their ever-changing size and movements began to play across our side of Mt. Whitney. Soon the clouds began to reflect the warm hues of the setting sun and we ate dinner watching the sunlight move up the face of Mt. Whitney and cling briefly to the peaks before disappearing. What an afternoon!

The following morning we woke to a hard frost, in fact, for a moment we both thought it had snowed. The ponds were frozen over and everything

Our campsite below the backside of Mt. Whitney. The summit (not visible) rises another 3,000 feet above these peaks.

that could be coated with thick white frost and ice was, including all our gear. I eventually coaxed the stove into lighting, and in between vigorous calisthenics to try and keep warm, cooked the last of our Canadian oatmeal for breakfast. I had saved it for today partially in celebration, because today we would reach the official end of the JMT, but mostly because the official end of the JMT was more than half a mile straight up on top of Mt.

Whitney at 14,491' and we would need all the calories we could get!

We broke camp in record time not so much because we wanted an early start, but because we were desperate to warm up and figured a brisk 3,000 foot vertical climb before lunch would do the trick. We were eventually right, but for the next couple of hours we were stuck in the shadow of Mt. Whitney, and it was mid morning before we took our jackets off (and even then there was still frost on our packs). Finally, about 11 a.m., after a relentless series of switchbacks, we reached Trail Crest Pass and the side trail to Whitney's summit.

From this junction the JMT turns abruptly north to follow a ridge line to the top of Mt. Whitney, while the main trail, now called the Mt. Whitney Trail, continues east toward the Whitney Portal Trailhead. The plan was to leave our packs here, hike the two and one-half miles to Whitney's summit, then return to claim our packs and head out toward Whitney Portal. So, after a short break we transferred some essentials into our fanny packs[19] and headed ever upward.

Now The Trail became really crowded with the combined influx of hikers approaching from the west as we had, and the great majority from the trailhead at Whitney Portal on the east. Most of this latter group of hikers were on a one day, 22-mile, round-trip kamikaze hike from the Whitney Portal Trailhead. They were the lucky winners from the daily lottery, and they had all started their day about 4 a.m., when they began mostly jogging up the 11-mile long trail, while gaining over a mile in altitude along the way.

Normally, competition from this level of athleticism would have been intimidating, but not today. We were on our "home turf," without packs, and within sight of victory — no one was passing us today! And no one did. The fact that we had been in daily training for almost a month certainly helped, but the real difference was that for most of that time we had been living above 10,000 feet. So, unless there was a resident of the

---

[19]Each of our packs had a small compartment that could be detached and converted to a fanny pack.

Himalayas among our fellow hikers, no one could have been as acclimated to the altitude as we were, and that turned out to be a good thing because at 14,000 feet there just isn't much in the way of oxygen, and every step upward soon became a conscious decision. In fact, the last 500 feet of the climb was reduced to a simple equation of will power and hemoglobin[20], and after all this time on the JMT, with the end literally in sight, nobody had a better combination of those two than we did. So, it was with enormous satisfaction, a bit of humility, and an unbelievable sense of relief that just before noon, after 29 days and more than 210 miles, we finally stepped onto the highest point in the Continental United States, Mt. Whitney.

We'd made it! Beneath us everywhere were mountain peaks, canyons, and in the far distance lay Owens Valley more than 10,000 feet *below* us! Almost as startling was the realization that, for thousands of miles in any compass direction, there was nothing *above* us but sky. Wow! Finally, it was a completely shared experience, certainly between Susie and me, but also with the 20 or so people who were at the summit with us. Each of them was almost as happy and as pleased with themselves as we were, and there was a wonderful feeling of camaraderie as everyone celebrated by jumping up and down, screaming victory shouts, giving and receiving congratulatory hugs, taking pictures, and my personal favorite — making cell phone calls[21].

Technically this was the end of the JMT, and though it was certainly thrilling to finally be here, there was a definite anticlimactic feel to the accomplishment because 11 miles of hard trail still lay between us and civilization. So, after thoroughly enjoying the view, standing in line to sign the official register kept there by the U.S. Forest Service, and sharing a

---

[20]The component in blood that carries oxygen. Becoming acclimated to high altitude is in large part a function of your body's ability to increase hemoglobin levels and thereby increase the amount of oxygen your blood can absorb.

---

[21]Yes, there was cell phone service on the top of Mt. Whitney, and we watched at least half a dozen different hikers making calls to friends and family to brag about their accomplishment. It was surreal. With the single exception of our layover day at Edison Lake, the most technology we'd seen in a month was our stove, and here we were surrounded by people surfing the Net!

wonderful ham sandwich that some poor guy had carried all the way to the top only to find he couldn't eat it due to altitude sickness, we headed back down The Trail and what would prove to be a very long day indeed.

Chapter 22

The end of The Trail

Our planned itinerary for the rest of the day had been left deliberately vague, but essentially we had agreed to hike out toward Whitney Portal as far as we could. To me this obviously meant we would hike *to* Whitney Portal and be done, because anything less meant that we would spend another night in the wilderness, and in the most fundamental sense that option just wasn't working for me. However, and I know how incredible this must sound, it would soon become apparent that Susie thought it meant we'd maintain our normal routine and stop by late afternoon, so we could spend another glorious night in our tent.

I'm not sure if I can adequately express just how little appeal spending another night in the wilderness held for me, nor how disappointed I was when my most recent assumption — that we'd jog back to where we had left our packs at Trail Crest Pass Junction — proved to be completely inaccurate. I had once again forgotten that we were going downhill, and nothing I could do or say was going to change Susie's slow and deliberate pace. Nevertheless, we did eventually arrive back at the junction where we had dropped our packs. Regrettably, and despite my fervent hopes to the contrary, no one had stolen them. So, after our too-short delight in hiking "pack-less," we put the heavy things back on, and by early afternoon we were heading down a narrow canyon over an often precarious two-mile switchback trail that was even steeper than our previous record drop down from Forester Pass. It was a difficult and scary descent all by itself, but what was about to really make this section memorable was just up ahead.

Rounding one of the interminable switchbacks about halfway down we entered a piece of The Trail that had actually been blasted into the vertical wall of the mountainside. Here the sun never shone and with the almost constant wind and freezing night time temperatures, the water that slowly seeped from the rocks had formed a thick sheet of ice that covered most of the width and length of the next 100 feet of trail. We were prepared for rain, lightning, gale force winds, and had even hiked through long patches of snow on some of the passes we'd crossed, but for some reason neither of us was mentally ready for ice sheets in late August, and we stood there in complete disbelief. A false step here would send you sliding over the edge and hurtling downwards for almost a 1,000 feet until both you and your fall would be broken by the jagged granite boulders that lay far below. Yikes!

Surely there must be another way around we both thought, but this was it. Looking down at Susie I could tell she was considering her options, and hiking all the way back to Yosemite Valley was currently in first place. It was another of those hard decisions with only bad choices, but she eventually took a deep breath, reached out and, with a death grip, grabbed firmly hold of the steel cable that provided a makeshift handrail, and s-l-o-w-l-y "white-knuckled" her way across. It was a terrifying crossing and both of us slipped on the ice more than once, but we eventually arrived at the other side, and by mid afternoon we had reached the bottom of the switchbacks. From there it was a short and mostly flat walk to Trail Camp, the first and by far the most popular of the only two designated camping areas on the Mt. Whitney Trail.

I had camped here more than 20 years ago with a group of friends during my first and only other ascent of Mt. Whitney. It had been late October, we were all miserable from altitude sickness, and the weather had turned to near blizzard conditions. It was a memorable experience, but not one that had endeared the place to any of us, and today it looked even worse than I remembered it. At just over 12,000 feet it was as desolate as our recent campsite near Forester Pass, but with none of its redeeming qualities. Instead of a lovely pristine lake and quiet solitude, Trail Camp was a barren dusty group-campsite, which every day was being used by almost 200 hikers. This extreme overuse gave it the appearance of a refuge camp, which was reinforced by the rows of chemical toilets that had been installed to handle all the human waste. Basically, it's an awful place overrun with people, smells, and outhouses, and it took only moments to decide that we wouldn't be staying here any longer than necessary. Still, after that last series of switchbacks, we both needed a rest. So, we paused just long enough to pump some water and eat what I calculated to be my 32nd Cliff Bar of the trip before heading out.

The plan now was to hike to Outpost Camp, about four miles down The Trail, and then decide whether to spend the night or hike out the rest of the way. By now there could be no confusion as to my preference, but Susie was fading fast, and I had agreed to remain silent and let her make the final decision. Accordingly, we continued down The Trail and arrived at the second campground just before 6 p.m. where we both immediately dropped our packs and plopped down on the nearest log. We'd been hiking for most of the last 11 hours, and had covered just over 12 miles. Almost as strenuous, we'd climbed up 3,000 feet to reach Mt. Whitney this morning, and hiked down more than 4,000 feet this afternoon. By any measurement this had been by far the hardest day on The Trail, and we were both exhausted.

Now, picture me sitting next to Susie on a log in Outpost Camp, while I *silently* looked at the map and saw that we were less than four miles from the end of The Trail — a distance we could cover in two hours! Now, imagine me looking up and *silently* watching Susie begin to remove from her pack the type of items that could only mean one thing — we were camping here tonight. "What!" I screamed to myself, "just two hours from civilization and she wants to stay here! Are you kidding me?"

Given the situation, I imagine Gandhi or some other great soul would have said something selfless and compassionate like, "Susie, you must be exhausted. Please, sit down and rest while I make dinner. After all, tomorrow will be a fine day for finishing our hike." Lamentably, that conversation never occurred, because, with the single exception of Susie, the only soul around was <u>mine</u>, and all it knew in the entire universe was that: *it had to get off The Trail!*

What happened next is still a matter of some confusion and differing interpretations, but it mostly happened like this. Still remembering my promise to remain silent about our camping choice for tonight, I just stood there — unable to move and not trusting myself to speak — watching Susie scurry about merrily preparing for a quick dinner and an early appointment with her sleeping bag. This went on for some minutes until she finally looked up and realized that I had stopped functioning. I was in the midst of an internal struggle as to whether I would escape to civilization for the night and return for Susie in the morning, or whether I would simply bang my head against a nearby tree until I achieved unconsciousness. Either choice presented problems, but it was definitely down to those two. In the end I'm not sure if it was her innate sense of compassion, her fear of being left alone in the wilderness, or her reluctance to deal with a head wound, but all by herself Susie came to the entirely correct conclusion that getting off The Trail was the right thing to do.

All right, so maybe it was just the prudent thing to do, and Susie's stony silence coupled with the abruptness of her departure did hint at a certain frustration with yours truly, but honestly I was too deliriously happy to worry. The next two hours were mostly a blur, partly because we were both so worn out, partly because it was starting to get dark, but mostly because of the blistering pace Susie had set. (If I had only known how fast she could walk when she was angry, I'd have put more energy into being obnoxious weeks ago!) On we marched without a stop and at 8:30 that night, just as darkness enveloped the Sierras, we arrived at Whitney Portal and the end of The Trail. 223 miles, seven major passes, and 29 days after we had started it was over, and we walked triumphantly into the light of the parking lot and the beginnings of civilization.

There are extraordinary events in everyone's life: leaving home to go to college, or holding your firstborn child, for example, when the feelings you experience are so intense that you actually sense portions of them leaking away, because no one can absorb that much emotion all at once. Looking back at the sign that marked the end of the John Muir Trail was one of those extraordinary events, and for a long time Susie and I just stood there overwhelmed and overjoyed. We had not only survived the JMT, we had managed to finish it!

With a mixture of deliverance and accomplishment, time seemed to stretch eternally. Everything was right in my world. Susie had started talking to me again, the JMT was *behind* us, and just up ahead stood a convenience store with its lights on, the door open, and a cooler full of beer. In that moment both of us knew that life just didn't get any better than this, and as we walked toward the light I couldn't help but wonder if the Universe with all its myriad twists and turns might not be benevolent after all.

Just as darkness enveloped the Sierras, we arrived at Whitney Portal and the end of The Trail

Epilogue

Looking back

We were off The Trail, but still a long way from home, and our first priority was to call our daughters, Amy and Bethany, to let them know that their parents were still alive. It was a comforting exchange for all of us. Everything back home was fine, but just before she hung up Bethany did mention in passing that a credit card had turned up missing, which she had therefore canceled as a precaution. "Would this be the same credit card that I have tucked safely in my pack?" I inquired. It was, of course, but she did have the number of the new credit card, which I carefully wrote down.

With that we said good-bye and promised to call back tomorrow once we figured out how we were getting home. "OK, smart guy," Susie asked after I'd hung up the phone, "You got us out two days early, so our ride home won't be here for another 48 hours. You spent all our cash back at VVR, and the only credit card we have between us has been canceled. What's your plan, Einstein?" It occurred to me then that a lesser man might have been intimidated by this list of seemingly insurmountable problems, but not me, and I smiled at Susie with absolute confidence. I had just survived the JMT, and unless there was a thunderstorm on the horizon or a bear in the parking lot, I wasn't afraid of anything.

So, with Susie following somewhat reluctantly behind me, I marched into the parking lot, and, with my pack still on and arms waving, stood in front of the first car that tried to leave. After all that time on The Trail I must have been a frightful sight, and both the driver and his passenger looked a little uneasy as they pulled to a stop. Trying to appear harmless I slowly walked around to the side of their car, where I bent down to make eye contact through the open window, pointed toward Susie and said, "Guys, we've been on the John Muir Trail for a month, and if we have to camp here in the parking lot tonight my wife is going to *kill* me. You've just got to give us a ride into town."

It worked! And in moments we were riding down the 12-mile windy mountain road toward Lone Pine, where, after expressing eternal gratitude to our chauffeurs, we got out at the first motel we came to. It may have cost me all the Karma I'll ever have in life, but that night I was on a roll and managed to get our room, dinner, and tomorrow's breakfast charged to a credit card I didn't have, but whose number I swore was good.

The next morning, after contacting the air charter service our plane arrived on schedule and in minutes we were flying over the Sierras toward home. Looking out the window I could see Mt. Whitney standing proudly above a string of mountain peaks that formed the backbone of the Sierras. Among those mountains was the route of the JMT and I could see pieces of familiar terrain fade into the northern horizon. Somewhere far to the north beyond view lay Yosemite Valley, where so long ago we had first left civilization behind. Intellectually I knew that our JMT hike was almost insignificant compared to those hearty individuals who every year complete thousands of trail-miles on the Pacific Crest Trail, or the Appalachian Trail, but emotionally I was still convinced that we had just circumnavigated the Earth.

On we flew, over mountain passes, across valleys and meadows, past lakes and streams — obstacles and distances that had taken us a month to cross, we now covered in less than one hour. One hour! It was absurd! Inside the plane I had a sense of being wrapped inside a cocoon of technology that was whisking me back to the *Everyday World* even as I looked down and watched the *Mountain World* — that place we had called home for the last month — disappear below me. It was surreal!

On we flew, while the entire Sierra Nevada Range disappeared behind us, and by lunchtime we were back home. Home: that comfortable, safe, warm, and reassuring place I had been dreaming about everyday for the last month, and I knew just how Dorothy must have felt when she found herself back in Kansas. "There's no place like home ...there's no place like home," I chanted as we became reacquainted with all the comforts and conveniences civilization offered — the shower, the couch, the refrigerator — I smiled at them all, and later I went to sleep and smiled all night long at our bed because it didn't smell like an old pair of gym shorts. It was wonderful!

The next morning we were both back at work trying to rejoin our previous lives and immediately realized what an uncomfortable process we were in for. Everything was still there mostly as we'd left it, but everything and everybody felt different. Just being apart from one another was different. On The Trail we had been practically joined at the hip for a month; now, our careers suddenly pushed us apart, and for the first week or so we called one another a couple of times each day just to check in. Even more startling was that by midweek, as the normal and predictable problems and stresses of the *Everyday World* began to appear, I caught myself wistfully remembering and occasionally even longing for our life on The Trail. What was I thinking?

Those first couple of weeks were awful, and for awhile I wondered if I was ever going to fit in anywhere. The problem, I finally recognized, was that the "truths" of these two worlds weren't lining up very well. In fact, they weren't lining up at all, and much of what I had previously taken for granted in my "normal life" was now being thrown into question. Of course, recognizing that life on The Trail is different from life in the *Everyday World* is hardly an epiphany, but having the stark contrast between these two worlds suddenly forced upon me eventually proved to be among life's most important lessons.

At first I tried to resolve all these issues by organizing everything into groups. Dehydrated food was in the bad group; fresh food was in the good group. OK! I thought this is easy: flush toilets — good; instant oatmeal — bad; but, soon these simplistic categories proved inadequate. Was it better to sit beside a beautiful meadow, or enjoy a cup of tea in the living room? Was hiking bad, and driving a car good? Couldn't you enjoy a beautiful sunset no matter where you were? Clearly, something else was going on here, and I eventually found myself remembering a conversation I had back when we were crossing Edison Lake.

I had been talking with the woman operating our ferry and remarked that I was sure her job must be very satisfying— pleasant working conditions, spectacular scenery, and happy customers. I had expected a simple nod of agreement, but instead she considered the question carefully, and finally answered by agreeing with my comment about the scenery and working conditions, but made a remarkable observation about her customers.

According to her, those hikers who were just starting their trip were almost always anxious — still thinking about work, in a hurry to reach the trailhead, worried they had forgotten something, and so on, but the people who were returning from the wilderness, after being away from civilization for a time, were relaxed and content. It was this second group, she said, the ones who had been desensitized to the demands and expectations of civilization, that you wanted to spend time with. They were on *Mountain Time*.

Mountain Time ...something felt right about that description, and for months I returned to this conversation over and over. Was this the real difference between these two groups of hikers and the worlds they represented? What exactly had the people on *Mountain Time* learned? The answer, I believe, is that they hadn't really "learned" anything at all. Rather, people on *Mountain Time* have simply been reconnected (often uncomfortably) to those simple and universal Truths that are inside each of us.

Life on The Trail automatically enrolls you in an advanced and intensive course on the difference between what <u>looks</u> important vs. what actually <u>is</u> important. The *Everyday World* is crowded with meetings, appointments, conflicts, obligations, and much more — events that demand our immediate attention because they appear to be important, but all too often are not. Cell phones, for example, literally scream at us with urgency and constantly interrupt our lives, yet almost never deliver anything that really matters. In the *Everyday World* it's easy to be confused about what is important.

On The Trail life is not cluttered with such confusions. Here there are few choices and even fewer conflicting priorities. Take food, for example. In the *Everyday World* dinner choices might easily include a few dozen restaurants or menu choices at the supermarket that number into the hundreds. Dinner choices on The Trail were a bit more limited. Basically, we ate whatever dehydrated meal had "floated" to the top of our bear canister. On The Trail (when you're losing ½ lb. per day) there is no confusion about menus, because you understand intuitively that it's not the choices that are important, it's the <u>eating</u> that's important.

The other BIG differentiator between these worlds is the ages-old concept of mindfulness — of being fully present and living in the moment. Almost everyone recognizes how useful and desirable this is, but in the *Everyday World*, with its endless demands and constant distractions, practicing mindfulness is notoriously difficult. How can you be in the moment, when you haven't a moment to spare? In contrast, on The Trail one lives by necessity almost entirely in the present. Trust me when I tell you that nothing, absolutely nothing, will focus the mind more than a lightning strike 200 yards from where you're standing — nothing! And, nothing will grab your attention like hauling an extra 45 pounds up and over a 12,000 foot pass. Whether you want to or not when you're on The Trail you're going to be engaged in a daily and continuous practice of living in the moment.

Now, I don't want to overstate any this, and I'm not suggesting for a moment that all conveniences are evil and that only hardship is "real." I assure you I am more keenly aware than ever of just how much I appreciate a myriad of modern conveniences (and I have a special fondness for indoor plumbing, central heating, and rapid transit, to name a few) but, each of these and thousands more 21st Century conveniences, have a nasty habit of disconnecting us from the world and insulating us from our fellow man.

I once read that life presents us with an unending series of lessons — the more painful the lesson the more we learn. For myself, I have found this to be so consistently and uncomfortably true that I sometimes wonder if life isn't actually some kind of metaphysical diner. I imagine that inside this "restaurant" lessons are prepared each day, and I can see myself standing in line waiting to be served. Across the counter stands the owner, who looks up as I approach and acknowledges me with an upturned eyebrow and the hint of a smile. His name is Life, and everyday he greets me in the same boisterous and cheerful voice, "Good Morning, Mike! Today we are serving lessons. Would you like yours the easy way or the hard way?"

Each time I hear this question I think to myself, "Wait! Didn't I get this wrong last time?" But, more often than not, just as the correct answer begins to surface, I hear myself answering, "I'd like mine the hard way, and while you're at it throw in a little angst on the side."

Life on The Trail was frequently like that — a continuing series of hard and often painful lessons, which seemed to mainly emphasize those simple yet often forgotten Truths like *Mountain Time*, mindfulness, and the interconnectedness of the Universe. To be sure there are Great Souls who seem never to forget these Truths, but there are others among us who apparently need to walk a very long way indeed before they remember.

In every way our journey on the JMT was an altogether extraordinary experience, and even though I fell far short of achieving enlightenment, nothing has ever taught me more. The hardships were real, but it was more than anything else a time of discovery, of insight, and of renewal, all wrapped up in the sublime beauty of the High Sierras. In short, "it was the best of times; it was the worst of times," and while I will tell you with conviction that I don't ever want to do it again, I would quickly add that I wouldn't have missed it for anything. Because every time I think about our adventure and all that we endured, and shared, and learned together, it makes me smile.

On top of Mt. Whitney. It was all downhill from here!

Appendix A
The Supporting Cast

The Supporting Cast
(in order of appearance)

Our trip, indeed our very survival, depended on the numerous re-supplies that were packed in by the following family and friends:

Amy Miner Filice, our oldest daughter, who's been backpacking since she was 9 years-old. She's hiked across the Sierras several times and to Half-Dome twice. She, along with Alisha and Hannah, hiked the first 25-miles of the JMT with us.

Alisha Crandall Pilkington, one of our "other" daughters, this was Alisha's first backpack trip. Part of the "3 Musketeers" (Alisha, Amy & Hannah) they have all been close friends since the 4th Grade.

Hannah Millard Rubalcava, another of our "other" daughters, she has actually been on more backpack trips with me than Amy. Hannah has been part of the family since she was 5 years-old.

Steve Miner, my brother, who went with me on my first Trans-Sierra backpack trip almost 15 years ago. He and his sons, Jake and Matt hiked the 35-miles from Red's Meadow to Lake Edison.

Jake Miner (left), our oldest nephew, and Matt Miner (right), our youngest nephew. Both have been on several backpack trips with me, but this was the first time either of them had hiked across the Sierras.

Dorothy Miner (left) our sister-in-law, and Tom Miner (right) our middle nephew, have both been on previous backpack trips with us, but this time they were part of the "transportation team." They drove around the Sierras to pick up Steve and the boys and to deliver our 3rd re-supply.

Bethany Miner, our youngest daughter, first climbed Half-Dome when she was 9 years-old. She's been across the Sierras and on numerous other backpack trips since. Worried that Susie and I were losing too much weight, she (along with Amy, Dorothy, and Tom) met us at Lake Edison with an ice chest full of extra food.

Mike Huston and his wife, Paula, hiked more than 30 miles when they accompanied us to Evolution Valley and delivered our 4th re-supply. Mike has been on several previous backpack trips with me helping to lead and keep track of several groups of high school students.

This was Paula Huston's first backpack trip ever. She took everything in stride including the ever-present thunder storms and our encounters with the snake and the bear in Evolution Valley. Besides that she carried in a fresh-baked apple pie that was to-die-for!

Bill Shearer and his friend, Paul, volunteered for the last and hardest re-supply. It took them a day and half to reach us at Woods Creek, and Susie and I were never so glad to see anybody in our lives. Besides our re-supply, Bill brought enough extra food to wait for a day (in case we were late) and I happily ate every bit of it in one delightful afternoon.

Paul Wilson, a good friend of Bill's, who, at almost the last minute, agreed to help Bill carry in all our gear when "the other guy" couldn't make it.

AppendixB
Trail Profile

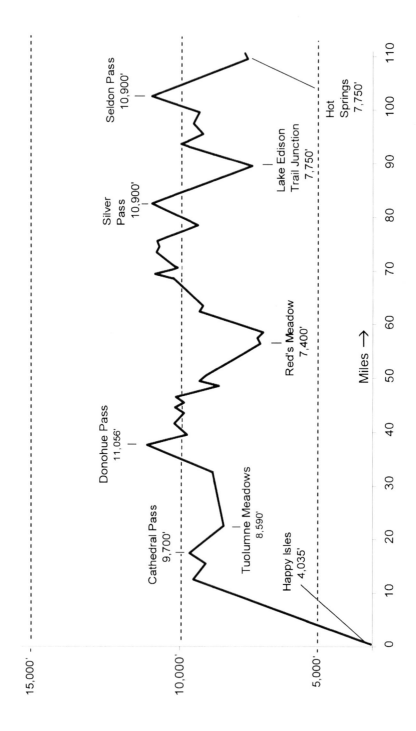

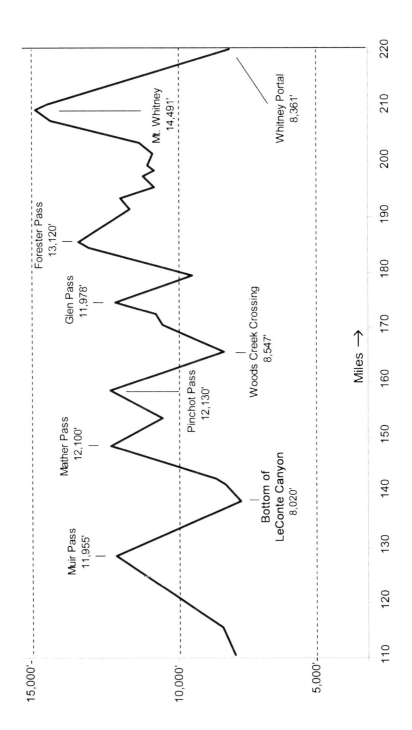

Muir Pass
11,955'

Mather Pass
12,100'

Glen Pass
11,978'

Forester Pass
13,120'

Mt. Whitney
14,491'

Pinchot Pass
12,130'

Bottom of
LeConte Canyon
8,020'

Woods Creek Crossing
8,547'

Whitney Portal
8,361'

Miles →

15,000'
10,000'
5,000'

110   120   130   140   150   160   170   180   190   200   210   220